大学英语选修课系列教材

COLLEGE ENGLISH
ELECTIVE COURSE SERIES

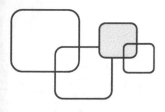

COLLEGE ENGLISH
ELECTIVE COURSE SERIES

《大学英语选修课系列教材》
COLLEGE ENGLISH ELECTIVE COURSE SERIES

语言文化类

Western Etiquette Culture

西方礼仪文化

主　编　欧　玲
副主编　（按姓氏笔画顺序）
平原春　许　骏
盛　荔

重庆大学出版社

内 容 提 要

本书作为大学英语选修课系列教材之一，旨在帮助即将走向社会的在校大学生了解一些基本的西方礼仪文化知识，未来在和外国友人的交往中更完美地展示自己，体现中国大学生良好的综合素质。本书一共分为八个章节，分别对日常交际礼仪、公共场合的行为礼仪、餐饮礼仪、着装礼仪、婚礼礼仪、丧葬礼仪、商务礼仪以及在西方礼仪文化中的禁忌进行了描述。每个章节分为六个部分，第一部分为相关内容的热身练习，第二部分对不同场合下人们应该遵守何种礼仪原则进行详细阐释，第三部分是针对相关内容设计的对话，第四部分是根据前几部分的内容设计的练习，第五部分为学生提供一些礼仪方面的幽默笑话，最后一部分是补充阅读材料，可供学生课外阅读了解更多的信息和知识。

本书可作为学生的课外阅读书籍，也可用作全校型人文素质选修课教材。

图书在版编目(CIP)数据

西方礼仪文化/欧玲主编．—重庆：重庆大学出版社，2008.9(2022.2 重印)
(大学英语选修课系列教材)
ISBN 978-7-5624-4622-4

Ⅰ．西…　Ⅱ．欧…　Ⅲ．礼仪—西方国家—高等学校—教材　Ⅳ．K891.26

中国版本图书馆 CIP 数据核字(2008)第 130656 号

大学英语选修课系列教材
西方礼仪文化
Western Culture & Etiquette
主　编　欧　玲
责任编辑：杨　琪　牟　妮　　版式设计：杨　琪
责任校对：夏　宇　　　　　　责任印制：赵　晟
*
重庆大学出版社出版发行
出版人：饶帮华
社址：重庆市沙坪坝区大学城西路 21 号
邮编：401331
电话：(023) 88617190　88617185(中小学)
传真：(023) 88617186　88617166
网址：http://www.cqup.com.cn
邮箱：fxk@cqup.com.cn (营销中心)
全国新华书店经销
POD：重庆新生代彩印技术有限公司
*
开本：720mm×960mm　1/16　印张：10.25　字数：189 千
2008 年 9 月第 1 版　　2022 年 2 月第 13 次印刷
ISBN 978-7-5624-4622-4　定价：39.00 元

总　序

我国的大学英语教学起步于20世纪80年代，经过20多年的发展，大学英语在教学水平、课程设置、教学方法、教学环境、师资队伍等各个方面都有了长足的进步和发展。但随着我国加入WTO和国民经济的快速发展，大学英语教学暴露出与时代要求不相称的一面。为适应现代社会对人才培养的实际需求，推动和指导大学英语教学改革，教育部于2003年颁布了《大学英语课程教学要求(试行)》(以下简称《要求》)，并于2007年结合对人才能力培养的新要求再次做了修订和调整，作为全国各高校组织非英语专业本科生英语教学的主要依据。

《要求》将大学阶段的英语教学分为一般要求、较高要求和更高要求三个层次，强调要贯彻分类指导、因材施教的原则，使英语教学朝着个性化的方向发展，要"将综合英语类、语言技能类、语言应用类、语言文化类和专业英语类等必修课程和选修课程有机结合，形成一个完整的大学英语课程体系，以确保不同层次的学生在英语应用能力方面得到充分的训练和提高"。这样，大力发展大学英语选修课就成了大学英语教学改革的重要课题。

大学英语选修课的开设不仅是《大学英语课程教学要求(试行)》精神的体现，也是《教育部财政部关于实施高等学校本科教学质量与教学改革工程的意见》(以下简称《意见》)的内在要求，《意见》将"学生的实践能力和创新精神显著增强"作为教学改革的重要目标之一，而大学英语教学要在这方面有所作为的话，必须注重培养学生的跨文化交际能力、文化素养和在全球化、信息化的背景下获取知识的能力，这显然是传统的大学英语教学和课程设置所不能胜任的。

近年来，全国许多高校纷纷进行了开设大学英语选修课的尝试，并取得了可喜的成绩。但是由于指导思想不明晰、教师知识结构单一和配套改革滞后等原因，在大学英语选修课的开设中出现了"因人设庙"，开课随意性强，开课种类单一，各门课程难易不均，课程测试不规范，学生对各门课程的兴趣差异过大等问题。大学英语选修课的开设迫切需要某种程度的规范与引导，需要更为科学地设置选修课程，确实达到《要求》和《意见》中提出的目标。

针对以上问题，我们认为，一套由成熟理念指引的、体系科学的、建立在选修课开设的成功实践基础之上的系列教材能够起到这种规范和引导作用。因此，重庆大学出版社组织来自全国各地的、在选修课开设方面走在前列的高校的专家和教师，在多次交流与反复论证的基础上，组织编写了这套"大学英语选修课系列教材"。该套教材具有以下明显的特点：

第一，教材体系科学、系统。系列教材以《大学英语课程教学要求（试行）》为指导，覆盖语言技能类、语言应用类、语言文化类和专业英语类四个板块，既注重语言基础知识的积累，也充分考虑对学生文化素质的培养，确保不同层次的学生在英语应用能力方面得到充分的训练和提高。

第二，坚持“实用、够用”的原则。在体例安排和内容选择上严格按照选修课的课时要求和学生水平的实际需要，力求精练，避免长篇累牍，在语言难度上体现了与英语专业同类教材的差别。

第三，注重知识与技能相结合，语言与文化相结合。在深入浅出地讲授知识的同时，结合课程内容尽可能多地为学生提供说与写的练习，在雕琢学生语言的同时，尽可能培养学生的跨文化交际能力和批判性思维能力。

第四，强调学生综合能力的培养。考虑到学生在选修课阶段可能不再修综合英语类的课程，各教材在主要训练与课程相关能力的基础上，适当补充了其他能力的训练内容。

第五，吸纳并总结近年来相关高校选修课开设的经验和成果。该套教材的参编者来自全国多所高校，多数教材是由开设该门课程最成功的、最受学生欢迎的学校和教师撰写，教材既吸纳了相关讲义的优点，又根据专家意见，按照学科要求和普遍情况进行了改编，在保证教材科学性的前提下，最大程度地体现了大学英语学生的选修取向。

选修课的开设是大学英语教学改革的重要发展方向，但是在改革中诞生的事物也必然不断地在改革中被重新定义，因此我们这套大学英语选修课教材的体系也将是动态的和开放的，不断会有新的教材被纳入，以反映大学英语教学改革在这方面最新的成功尝试。相信随着教学改革不断走向深入，我们的教材体系也将日臻完善。

总主编

2008 年 1 月

前　言

中国自古就是一个礼仪之邦，礼仪文化可谓博大精深。随着经济全球化、一体化和跨文化交际的进程，越来越多的人认识到西方礼仪文化在我们的对外交往中的重要性。礼仪在人际交往中是一个衡量个人文明的准绳，它反映着一个人的交际技巧和应变能力，还反映一个人的气质风度、阅历见识、道德情操、精神风貌。充分了解西方礼仪文化不仅能让我们在对外交际活动中充满自信，处变不惊，还能使自己更好地向外国友人表达自己的尊重、敬佩、友好和善意，增进彼此的信任和了解，进而造就和谐、完美的人际关系，取得事业的成功。

礼仪和文化紧密相关，不同国度在文化上也有很大的差异。本书所述的礼仪文化主要集中在欧美国家，也谈及一些在国际交往中的惯常规则。本书共分八个章节，分别对日常交际礼仪、公共场合的行为礼仪、餐饮礼仪、着装礼仪、婚礼礼仪、丧葬礼仪、商务礼仪以及在西方礼仪文化中的禁忌进行了描述。每个章节则分为六个部分：第一部分为相关内容的热身练习；第二部分对不同场合下人们应该遵守何种礼仪原则进行详细阐释；第三部分是针对相关内容设计的对话，目的是使学生不但能了解礼仪文化，也能在有关场合使用恰当的英语表达；第四部分是根据前几部分内容设计的练习；第五部分为礼仪文化方面的幽默、笑话；最后一部分是补充阅读材料，可供学生课外了解更多的信息和知识。本书编写针对的是即将走向社会的在校大学生，希望此书能帮助我们的大学生了解基本的西方礼仪文化知识，将来在和外国友人的交往中更完美地展示自己，体现中国大学生良好的综合素质。

本书可作为学生的课外阅读书籍，也可用作全校型人文素质选修课教材使用。

编　者

2008 年 6 月

Table of Contents

Brief Introduction to Etiquette / 1

Unit 1
The Etiquette of Daily Personal Communication / 6

Unit 2
The Etiquette of Behavior in Public Places / 26

Unit 3
The Etiquette of Dining / 44

Unit 4
The Etiquette of Dressing / 63

Unit 5
The Etiquette at Wedding Ceremony / 81

Unit 6
The Etiquette in Funeral Ceremony / 96

Unit 7
The Etiquette of Business / 112

Unit 8
The Taboos in Western Culture and Etiquette / 132

参考文献 / 153

Brief Introduction to Etiquette

1. *What is etiquette*?

Etiquette is a set of practices and forms which are followed in a wide variety of situations; many people consider it to be general social behavior or a branch of decorum (礼节), which is a code that governs the expectations of social behavior, according to the contemporary conventional norm within a society, social class, or group. Usually unwritten, it may be codified(变成法典) in written form.

Etiquette codes prescribe and restrict the ways in which people interact with each other, based on respect for other people and the accepted customs of a society.

Modern etiquette codifies social interactions with others, such as:

- Greeting relatives, friends and acquaintances with warmth and respect
- Refraining from insults and inquisitive curiosity
- Offering hospitality to guests
- Wearing clothing suited to the occasion
- Contributing to conversations without dominating them
- Offering assistance to those in need
- Eating neatly and quietly
- Avoiding disturbing others with unnecessary noise
- Following established rules of an organization upon becoming a member
- Arriving promptly when expected
- Comforting the bereaved(丧失亲属的人)
- Responding to invitations promptly
- Accepting gifts or favors with humility and acknowledging them promptly with thanks (e.g. a thank-you card)

2. *Why does etiquette need to exist*?

It is the practice with certain people to sneer at the word "etiquette", and to claim that it merely means a foolish support to some silly customs which in themselves have no meaning or use. This is a misunderstanding which a little thoughtful consideration will remove. Since the human beings came into the world, the interaction has become essential for a variety of purposes. They learned to behave in ways that made life easier and more pleasant. Then early civilizations developed rules for proper social conduct, which became early etiquettes.

Some people consider etiquette to be an unnecessary restriction of freedom of personal expression; others consider such free spirits to be unmannerly and rude. For instance, wearing blue jeans to a wedding in a cathedral may be an expression of the guest's freedom, but may also cause the bride and groom to suspect that the guest in jeans is expressing amusement or disrespect towards them and their wedding. Etiquette may be enforced in pragmatic ways: "No shoes, no shirt, no service" is a notice commonly displayed outside stores and cafés in the warmer parts of North America. Others feel that a single, basic code shared by all makes life simpler and more pleasant by removing many chances for misunderstandings.

Violations of etiquette, if severe, can cause public disgrace, and in private hurt individual feelings, create misunderstandings or real grief and pain, and can even develop into murderous rage. Many family feuds(不和、争执) have their beginnings in trivial etiquette violations that were blown out of proportion. In the ancient Hindu(印度的) epic (史诗) *Mahabharata*, the entire world-destroying conflict between the armies of two clans (宗族) begins when one ruler, Duryodhana, commits a couple of minor faux pas(失礼) at his cousin's castle, and is impolitely made fun of for it. One can reasonably view etiquette as the minimal politics required to avoid major conflict in polite society, and as such, an important aspect of applied ethics.

Maybe Emily Post, a United States author who promoted what she considered "proper etiquette" has presented us a sound reason for etiquette: "There is no reason why you should be bored when you can be otherwise. But if you find yourself sitting in the hedgerow(灌木篱墙) with nothing but weeds, there is no reason for shutting your eyes and seeing nothing, instead of finding what beauty you may in the weeds." Beauty is something nobody can resist in the world.

3. *How did etiquette come into being*?

Much of today's formal etiquette originated in the French royal court during the 1600-1700's. Louis XIV's gardener at Versailles (凡尔赛宫) was faced with a serious problem: he could not stop members of the nobility from trampling (踩踏) about in the delicate areas of the King's garden. He finally attempted to dissuade their unwanted behavior by posting signs called etiquets which warned them to "Keep off the Grass". When this course of action failed, the King himself had to issue an official decree (政令、法令) that no one could go beyond the bounds of the signs. Later, the name "etiquette" was given to a ticket for court functions that included rules regarding where to stand and what to do. Another saying from Wikipedia is the nobles who lived at court did not work, and so they developed elaborate social customs mostly to avoid becoming bored. The nobles drew up a list of proper social behavior and called it etiquette. This code of behavior soon spread to other European courts and eventually was adopted by the upper classes throughout the Western world.

The word "etiquette" has evolved with the development of the society, but in many ways it still means "Keep off the Grass". Remaining within the flexible boundaries of civil behavior allows relationships and us to grow like flowers in Louis' garden. Moreover, it lets us present ourselves with confidence and authority in all areas of our professional and personal life.

Over the years, people were expected to follow an increasingly complicated set of rules. Many of the rules seem silly today. In Western countries in the 1800's, a young man could not speak to a young woman he knew until she had first acknowledged him. Little girls curtsied (行屈膝礼) and little boys bowed when introduced to someone. Not many years ago, when a young man and a young woman went out on a date, she was expected to sit quietly in the car while he walked around it to open her door and help her out.

Since the 1960's, manners have become much more relaxed. Etiquette today is based on treating everyone with the same degree of kindness and consideration, and it consists mostly of common sense. It is helpful to know some rules about how to behave in certain situations—if only because this makes life more comfortable for you and makes you more self-confident in social situations.

4. *What's the relationship between etiquette and culture*?

It goes without saying that etiquette is heavily dependent on culture; what is excellent etiquette in one society may be a shock in another. Etiquette evolves within culture. Etiquette can vary widely between different cultures and nations. In China, a person who takes the last item of food from a common plate or bowl without first offering it to others at the table may be regarded impolite. In most European cultures a guest is expected to eat all of the food given to them, as a compliment to the quality of the cooking. Learning etiquette can be very challenging for people who are new to a particular culture, and even old hands sometimes have a rough time.

An etiquette may reflect an underlying ethical code, or it may grow more as a fashion, as in 18th century Britain where apparently pointless acts like the manner in which a tea cup was held became associated with the upper class. Like "culture", it is a word that has gradually grown plural, especially in a multi-ethnic society with many clashing expectations. Thus, it is now possible to refer to "an etiquette" or "a culture", realizing that these may not be universal. In Britain, though, the word etiquette has its roots in the 18th century, becoming a universal force in the 19th century to the extent that it has been described as the one word that properly describes life during the reign of Queen Victoria.

Etiquette is a topic that has occupied writers and thinkers in all sophisticated societies for long, beginning with a behavior code by Ptahhotep, a vizier (高官) in ancient Egypt's Old Kingdom during the reign of the Fifth Dynasty king Djedkare Isesi (ca. 2414-2375 B. C.). All known literate civilizations, including ancient Greece and Rome, developed rules for proper social conduct. Confucius included rules for eating and speaking along with his more philosophical sayings. Early modern conceptions of what behavior identifies a "gentleman" were codified in the 16th century, in a book by Baldassare Castiglione, Il Cortegiano ("The Courtier"); its codification of expectations at the Este court remained in force in its essentials until World War I. Louis XIV established an elaborate and rigid court ceremony, but distinguished himself from the high bourgeoisie (资产阶级) by continuing to eat stylishly with his fingers.

In the UK, Debrett's is considered by many to be the arbiter (仲裁者) of etiquette;

their guides to manners and form have long been the last word among polite society. Traditional publications such as *Correct Form* have recently been updated to reflect contemporary society and new titles *Etiquette for Girls and Manners for Men* act as guides for those who want to combine a modern lifestyle with traditional values.

In the American colonies, Benjamin Franklin and George Washington wrote codes of conduct for young gentlemen. The immense popularity of advice columns and books by Letitia Baldrige and Miss Manners shows the currency of this topic. Even more recently, the rise of the Internet has necessitated the adaptation of existing rules of conduct to create *Netiquette*, which governs the drafting of email, rules for participating in an online forum, and so on.

In Germany, there is an "unofficial" code of conduct, called the Knigge, based on a book of high rules of conduct written by Adolph Freiherr Knigge in the late 18th century entitled exactly *Über den Umgang mit Menschen* (On Human Relations). The code of conduct is still highly respected in Germany today and is used primarily in the higher society.

There are so many different cultures all over the world, so it is impossible to touch every special one under different cultures. In the following chapters, the etiquette in western society (especially English speaking counties and some western European countries) will be mainly focused on. Actually, there are a lot of codes that are now shared worldwide.

Etiquette may be handled as a social weapon. The outward adoption of the superficial mannerisms of an in-group, in the interests of social advancement rather than a concern for others, is a form of snobbism(势利), lacking in virtue.

Unit 1

The Etiquette of Daily Personal Communication

Part I Lead-in Exercises

1. ***There are some English idioms used to describe the daily communication, please match the idioms from* 1) *to* 6) *with the meanings from A to F respectively.***

1) Do as the Romans do.
2) If you lie down with dogs, you will get up with fleas.
3) Those who live in glass houses should not throw stones.
4) Old habits die hard.
5) Man proposes, God disposes.
6) It is a sin to steal a pin.

A. You will be influenced by the people with whom you stay gradually.
B. When you are in a new place, you should follow the local people's practice.
C. You'd better avoid making a mistake, even it is a minor one.
D. One may plan a thing carefully, but there are many other factors beyond his control contribute to the success of it.
E. Don't treat others the way in which you hate being treated.
F. It is very hard for a person to quit his old habit.

2. ***Choose one response from the following answers to complete each of the short dialogues which happen in daily communication.***

1) — Excuse me. May I use your dictionary, please?

— ________.

A. No, thanks.

B. It doesn't matter.

C. Sorry, I'm referring a word in it now.

D. That's nothing.

2) — You are very beautiful in this dress?

— ________.

A. No, not at all. B. Thanks.

C. Where, where. D. You are flattering me.

3) — If you're free this afternoon, how about shopping together?

—________

A. All right. B. Not at all. C. See you later. D. Bye.

4) — Do you mind if I use the computer here?

—________. It's for Mr. Ford.

A. Not at all. B. Never mind. C. I'm sorry you can't. D. Of course not.

3. ***Suppose all of the following situations take place in western countries, how will you behave? Choose appropriate answers and discuss them with your partners.***

1) If a porter is offering help of carrying your heavy luggage to your room in a hotel when you travel in Europe, what should you do?

A. Say "thank you" only.

B. Write a letter of compliment to the manager of the hotel.

C. Say "thank you" and give him a tip when you get into your room.

D. Refuse his help rudely.

2) You meet your professor when you are together with your friend who is of the same age as you. It is polite to introduce ________.

A. your professor to your friend first.

B. neither of the two.

C. your friend to your professor first.

D. them to each other without mentioning their relationship with you.

3) You are a guest in your American friend's home. You have drunk enough coffee when your friend is going to refill your cup again. What should you do?

A. Cover your cup with one hand and say "No".

B. Say "No, thank you".

C. Say "Yes, please" and accept his offer with reluctance.

D. Say "Ok, let me refill it by myself".

4) You received a birthday gift from your intimate friend. What should you do in his or her presence?

A. Say "Thank you!" and unwrap it at once.

B. Say "You shouldn't have bought it, you have wasted your money."

C. Say "It must be very expensive." and refuse to accept.

D. Accept it calmly and collectedly, then unwrap it after the friend's leaving.

5) You received an invitation that has the letters R. S. V. P.. What should you deal with it?

A. Reply in time.　　B. Refuse in person.

C. Do nothing.　　D. Accept it in your heart.

Part II The Etiquette of Daily Personal Communication

"Etiquette requires us to admire the human race." —Mark Twain

1. *Daily Greetings*

It is polite and habitual for western people to greet each other when meeting, *Good morning*, *Good afternoon*, *Good evening* are often used for formal greetings. The most usual answer to *Good morning*, etc, is to say the same. Less formal greetings are *Hello* or *Hi*. When leaving, people say *Goodbye* in a formal situation, and *Goodbye*, *Bye*, *Bye-bye* or *See you* in an informal situation.

For asking each other about their health. *How are you* is the commonest expression and common answers are: *Very well, thank you* or *Fine, thank you*; *Very well (or Fine), thanks* is less formal. After people have responded to *How are you*, they often repeat (*And*) *how are you*? Or less formally, add *and you*?

As far as the titles used when greeting, using first names is widespread, even when adults are addressed by children. But professionals like doctors, lawyers, teachers and

bosses are often called by last names. Titles that precede the last name include *Mr*, *Mrs*, *Miss* and *Ms* which is used when a women's marital status is not sure to you. In some formal or respect-required situations, *Sir* is used independently when a man's name is not known to you and *Madam* is used when a women's name is unknown. In some places or certain occasions, people also smile and greet to strangers. which is quite different from the manners of Chinese.

2. *Introduction*

An introduction is called for in the occasion when people would feel unnatural without it.

When two people are introduced by the third party, the common practice is: a man is introduced to a woman first; for example, "*Mrs. Faud, this is my colleague, Mr. Hower*"; a younger person to an elder person; a subordinate to a superior; a child to an adult, a newly-joined person to the members of the group, etc. A question like "*Mrs. Golden, may I introduce my friend Tim White or Mr. Eric, may I present my daughter Ketty?* " is the most polite form of introduction. People usually shake hands when first introduced. In informal situations, especially in North America, introductions can be made by simply saying: "*This is (name).*" "*Hi*" or "*Hello*" is often held as a response in this informal situation.

When introducing someone, give some brief appropriate information about that person. Sometimes at a meeting or gathering it is all right to introduce oneself to others present.

Till the ending of a conversation with a new acquaintance, it is pleasant to say, "*good-bye, it was nice meeting you.*" Some expressions wishing the person a good time or good luck like "*enjoy your staying here*" might be added. They are helpful to make an appropriate ending.

3. *Hands-shaking*

Hands-shaking is a widely adopted practice which comes from European countries. It sometimes naturally accompanies an introduction, or it happens when friends or acquaintances meet after not having seen each other for a long time or people part in business and other formal situations. For people who meet quite often, they may just smile or nod to each other instead of shaking hands. Friends and family members often hug or kiss on the cheek when they see each other (typical of the United States).

Between persons of the same sex, it is usual for the older to hold his hand out first; between different sexes, it is the woman who initiates her hand or shows the intention of a hand-shaking; between two persons of different ranks, it is the one with higher rank. If others offer to shake hands, it is not appropriate to reject directly. When a female prefers not to shake hands, she may just bow slightly.

Offering a firm handshake which lasts for 3-5 seconds upon greeting and leaving is proper in business or other formal occasions. One should avoid shaking hands with more than one person one time or shaking hands with one but looking elsewhere or another person. Maintaining good eye contact during your handshake is a polite manner. If you are meeting several people at once, keep eye contact with the person you are shaking hands with, until you are moving on the next person.

Ervin & Lena Dassow
Family Reunion

Date: June 15, 2002
Time: 11:00am to 6:00pm

Where: Bluhm Park in Muskego
S77 W13607 McShane Dr.

Games, Raffles, Prizes, Food and Fun

Please RSVP:

Pam Shackelford
Phone: (414) 476-7815
Email: Pam_Shackelford@jeffersonwells.com

Jeanie Birlingmair
Phone: (262) 742-3978
Email: pinewood@netwurx.net

Please bring a dish to pass

4. *Invitations*

Invitations may be in the form of a telephone call, a printed card, or a written note. The choice of form may depend on the size and for reality of the event and the time available for preparing it. For example, you might use the telephone to invite a few friends to dinner. But for invitations to formal occasions such as dinners, dances or weddings, they should be given in advance, generally speaking, three or more weeks before the occasion, allowing the invitee enough time to reply. Thus hasty is avoided.

Formal invitations are either hand-written or typed on double sheets of quality paper to show the dignity of the occasion. Standard and fixed patterns are often used and the writer may write little on his own.

If a married person is invited, his or her spouse should also be included in a formal invitation in most cases. When a family with young children is invited, if the inviter intends to invite all the children, all the children's first names should be listed on the invitation, instead of "and family". Otherwise, "adults only" is written on the invitation.

It is important to reply as soon as possible to any invitation by telephone or by mail. If the invitation is given in person or by telephone, you can either say Yes or No at once or should call back with your answer within a day or two at most. If the invitation has the letters R. S. V. P. (an abbreviation for the French phrase "Repondez, s'il vous plait", which means "Please reply") on it, a reply in time is required.

Example* 1: *Formal Invitation

Dr. and Mrs. Richard Wilbur
request the pleasure of
Mr. and Mrs. Mark Strand's
company at dinner
on Thursday, July the twenty-second
at eight o'clock
200 Forest Avenue

Example* 2: *Acceptance to a formal invitation

Mr. and Mrs. Mark Strand
accept with pleasure
Mr. and Mrs. Richard Wilbur's
kind invitation to dinner
on Thursday, July the twenty-second
at eight o'clock

Example** 3 : **Decline to a formal invitation

Mr. and Mrs. Mark Strand
regret that previous engagement
prevents their accepting
Mr. and Mrs. Richard Wilbur's
kind invitation to dinner
on Thursday, July the twenty-second

5. *Paying a Visit*

A visit seldom happens before making an appointment which should be made in advance. If an appointment is made hastily, the person invited may decline the invitation, since the invitation may clash with a previous arrangement or he may guess he is not paid proper respect.

Who are these people, and what are they doing in my home?

When invited to a dinner or something alike, you should arrive exactly at the time according to the appointment or given in the invitation, sometimes you may be a few minutes later (but not beyond a quarter). Punctuality is highly appreciated in western culture. If one is not prompt, he may be regarded as ill-mannered or not fully responsible. You should not go to the other extreme to arrive much early also, because your host or hostess will probably be busy doing other things and not be ready to meet you earlier. Your earlier arrival may interfere with his or her arrangement and cause inconvenience.

When you are invited to a dinner in somebody's house, it is advised to bring some gifts, such as a bunch of flower for the hostess, a box of choc or candy, a bottle of wine, the value of the gift depends on the true relationship between you and the inviter.

Keeping good eye contact during social conversations shows interest, sincerity and confidence, but intense eye contact is a negative sign.

While talking, keep a moderate space is comfortable to speakers, if too close, a safety space is broken, if it is too far, an indifferent air is on. Keeping about two feet away is a common practice.

If something will be offered by the host or hostess, being frank and direct may bring comfort to both the guest and the host.

If you intend to do something that might have an effect on the people around, ask permission from them, say, before lighting a cigarette or cigar, due to health concerns, you may or may not be given permission.

It is not proper to stay in other's house for a long period of time, unless you are very close friends or you are invited to stay overnight. Generally speaking, guests tend to leave an acceptable period to both parties after diner, say, one or two hours, too late or too early are considered impolite and rude.

6. *Thanks*

Before leaving any house in which you are a guest, you must find your hostess and thank her. It will be more appropriate for you to write her a letter to thank her again after you go back home. This letter is called "bread and butter note". Make the note sound as if you were talking to your host or hostess in person.

Thank-you notes are also written for a gift, a favor, or some other hospitality. The purpose of writing thank-you letters is to express one's thanks or appreciation to others for having got their gifts, help or other favors.

The key point of a thank-you letter is sincerity. Equally importantly, it should be sent as soon as possible. And don't save words to express your sincerity and heart-felt appreciation in a thank-you letter.

***Example* 1**

Dear Rice,

Thank you so much for the pretty crystal vase you and Truman sent! It's exact the style I want and one of the nicest gifts I have received on our anniversary. How considerate of you to select it for us!

Stephen sends thanks too; can you come soon and see how lovely the crystal vase looks on our dining table? Call me.

Very truly yours

Example 2

Maureen, dear

I'm writing to say thank you for the pleasant weekend I spent at your lovely house. I not only had a good time, but I enjoyed the wonderful food!

Please give my regards to your mother, Ivy, who cooked delicious meals for me. More hearty thanks to you and your family for inviting me.

Thank you again for your hospitality.

Yours Eunice

7. *Giving and receiving Gifts*

Giving and receiving gift is a common practice and necessary etiquette in social communication, it helps establish and maintain relationships. Gifts are always exchanged between friends, family members, colleagues and acquaintances on the following festivals: Saint Valentine's Day, Easter Sunday and Christmas, etc. Western people seldom send and receive gifts on New Year's Day, because it is quite close to Christmas.

There are also some occasions calling for giving and receiving gift: bridal shower, wedding, baby shower, birthday, house warming party, visiting one's home, visiting a patient, funeral and so on.

It is not considered polite for a male to give too expensive or too personal a gift (such as clothing) to a female unless they are very close. When invited to a meal by friends, guests often bring a bottle of wine, a bouquet of flowers, a box of candy or other small gifts.

When presenting a gift, the giver may tell the receiver how careful he picks the gift and it is a wonderful one. Sometimes, a certain gift is required by the potential receiver, for instance, before a bridal shower, the theme of it may be set as "kitchen shower", so most of the gifts for the future bride should be kitchen wares.

When a gift is received, open it at the presence of the giver, saying words like "*thank you*" "*I really appreciate it*" "*it's so pretty*" to show you gratitude and appreciation to the giver. If the gift is food, unwrap it and share it with the people present.

Gifts should be reciprocated; it is not acceptable to receive gifts without offering something in return.

8. *Making a Phone Call*

The using of telephone is now so popular throughout the world that it has become an indispensable part of some people's daily life and work, especially with the development of all types of mobile phones. Talking on telephone call requires one to be polite, orderly and natural so as to make effective use of it.

The time chosen during a day for a call may not violate the general rule. It is not conventional to call someone very early in the morning, maybe he is busy with his daily routine or breakfast, a call comes in this time indicates it requires immediate handling. The same message is conveyed when a call arrives very late in the evening.

When speaking over the telephone, courtesy is as important as when having a face-to-face talk. The caller should say "*this is ... speaking*, *may I speak to* ... ?" to tell his or her name first before asking for the person desired. The person on the other end of the wire should answer the phone with a pleasant "*hello*".

If the person wanted is not available at that moment or is out, the person who answers the phone should inform the caller of the information and suggest other alternative by saying something like, "*He is in a conference. Can I get him to call you back as soon as possible*?" When taking a message, the caller's detailed information, should be taken, including caller's full name and telephone number, the time of the call and sometimes the purpose of the call, if he is willing to state.

If one dials a wrong number by accident or for unknown reason, he should not hang up without a word, "*I am sorry*" or "*please forgive me*" is expected before hanging up.

9. *Gentlemanlike Manners*

In the past, males were regarded as the stronger and dominant sex, so they were obliged to protect and help the "weaker" sex, females.

Many etiquettes are expected to be performed toward women by men: helping women on and off their coat, opening doors for them, pulling table chairs before and after dinner for women, allowing a lady to go before him, letting women getting on a train or bus first, steering them around by the elbow, walking on the outside when with a woman. The list may go on.

But nowadays, many self-sufficient women guess such favor and protection may offend their independence and confidence. Most men still continue to perform the conventional courtesies, yet both parties don't attach the same importance to it as before.

10. *Tipping*

Tipping seems never come to our mind when we are in China, but if you study, work or travel abroad, it is a necessity in daily life. Tipping practice varies considerably from country to country, from one place of a same country to another, from one occasion to another.

Generally speaking, 15 to 20 percent of the bill is a common tip to westerns. But it may change according to the different situations. For instance, you may give a more generous tip to a doorman in a luxurious hotel than that you give to a doorman in an ordinary one. The quarter (25 cents) is very welcome in using since it is the normal tipping coin for minor services.

You are expected to offer tip to the following people after they provide service: waiters or waitresses, taxi drivers, porters, doormen, barbers, shoeshine persons, delivery people to your door, tour guides, cleaners, etc. Because many of them are underpaid by their employers, tips is an indispensable part of their income, so if you deny giving tips, their interests will be violated.

In some restaurants or hotels, the service fee is included in the bill and you need not pay extra tip any more.

Words and Expressions

alternative	*n.* 二中择一，可供选择的办法，事物
clash with	冲突

crystal	*a.* 水晶的
precede	*v.* 在……之前,先于
marital	*a.* 婚姻的
subordinate	*n.* 下属
Easter Sunday	复活节
house warming party	暖屋宴会
professional	*n.* 专业人员
punctuality	*n.* 准时
reciprocate	*v.* 互给，酬答，互换

Part III Sample Dialogues

Sample Dialogue 1: Expressing Thanks

Wang Ming: I don't know how to thank you for giving me such a fine farewell party. I shall never forget your kindness.

Mr. White: Never mind, what impressed you most during your stay here?

Wang Ming: Well... everyone was so kind and generous... when I'm enjoying myself like this with your people; I feel I never want to leave your town.

Mr. white: I hope you will come here again some time.

Sample Dialogue 2: Refusing/ Receiving an Invitation

Peter: Hello!

Tom: Hello! This is Tom speaking. Is that Peter speaking?

Peter: Yes. How are you, Tom?

Tom: Fine. How about you, Peter?

Peter: Oh, I'm very well, but very busy.

Tom: But you've finished your exams now, haven't you?

Peter: Yes, but I've got a lot of things to do.

Tom: How about coming out with us to play football tomorrow?

Peter: Oh, I've promised to see my roommate off at the airport.

Tom: What about the weekend? Are you free then?

Peter: Such a pity. I've arranged to visit my tutor this weekend.

Tom: Oh, how busy you are! What about next week, some time?

Peter: That would be great! Oh, I have to hang up now. Someone wants to use the phone. So see you next week.

Tom: OK. I will call you to make sure of the exact date. Bye.

Sample Dialogue 3: Introduction

Wang Ming: Please allow me to introduce a friend of mine, Mr. Johnson.

Mr. White: I've long heard about your name!

Mr. Johnson: Nice to meet you.

Mr. White: I am glad to have the honor of your acquaintance.

Mr. Johnson: I hope we'll be able to meet often in the future. This is my business card.

Mr. White: I am very happy to meet you. Here is mine.

Mr. Johnson: I've heard a great deal about you, but I did not expect to meet you today.

Sample Dialogue 4: Making a Phone call

A: Hello!

B: Hello! May I speak to Mrs. Mary Sharp, please?

A: May I ask who is calling?

B: My name is Gorge Winster. I've just arrived in New York from Canada.

A: Oh! Mr. Winster. How nice! This is Mrs. Mary Sharp. I've heard Golden mention your name but we didn't know you'd have arrived so soon. How long will you stay in New York?

B: About a week or so. And then I plan to go to San Francisco for a few days.

A: Oh, that's nice! Is there a number where I can reach you?

B: I'm staying at the New York Holiday Inn. The number is 456-2300. My room number is 1209.

A: How about spending an evening together?

B: That'll be very nice.

A: When is it most convenient to call you?

B: Anytime between 7 and 9 p. m. would be fine.

A: OK! I'll call you.

B: Then I'll be talking to you soon. Bye.

A: Bye-bye.

Part IV Follow-up Practice

1. ***Suppose you receive a wonderful birthday gift from an American friend. Write a thank-you note to express your thanks.***

2. ***Role play: Wang Ling is invited to a dinner at a foreign friend Mike Fernan's home. Make up a dialogue for the three: Wang Ling, Mike and his wife who is a stranger to Wang Ling.***

3. ***Compare western etiquette of daily personal communication with our Chinese practice. Make a list of some differences.***

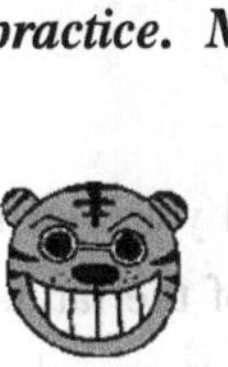

Part V Reading for Fun

A Wild Guess

It was the end of the school year, and a kindergarten teacher was receiving gifts from her pupils. The florist's(种花人) son handed her a gift. She shook it, held it overhead, and said, "I bet I know what it is. Flowers." "That's right!" the boy said, "But, how did you know?" "Oh, just a wild guess," she said. The next pupil was the sweet shop owner's daughter. The teacher held her gift overhead, shook it, and said, "I bet I can guess what it is. A box of sweets." "That's right, but how did you know?" asked the girl. "Oh, just a wild guess," said the teacher. The next gift was from the son of the liquor storeowner. The teacher held he package overhead, but it was leaking. She touched a drop off the leakage(渗漏) with her finger and put it to her tongue. "Is it wine?" she asked. "No," the boy replied, with some excitement. The teacher repeated the process, tasting a larger drop of the leakage. "Is it champagne?" she asked. "No," the boy replied, with more excitement. The teacher took one more big taste before declaring, "I give up, what is it?" With great glee(快乐), the boy replied, "It's a puppy!"

Part VI Supplementary Reading

1. *Talking Manners*

All of us can change our talking behavior to fit the different situations. When we speak with close friends, for example, we are free to interrupt them and we will not be offended if they interrupt us. When we speak to our employers, however, we are inclined to hear them out before saying anything ourselves. If we don't make such adjustments, we are likely to get into trouble. We may fail to accomplish our purpose and we are almost sure to be considered ill-manners or worse. Here are some tips of ideal conversation manners for you to practice:

• ***Be a Careful Speaker***

If you are one of those who dread meeting strangers because you are afraid you won't be able to think of anything to say, you might do well to remember that most of the faults of conversation are committed not by those who talk little, but by those who talk too much. The person whom most people love to sit next to is a sympathetic listener who makes others want to talk.

• ***The Popular "Middle Road"***

People who talk too easily are apt (倾向于) to talk too much and at times imprudently (鲁莽地). On the other hand, the "man of silence", who never speaks except when he has something worthwhile to say, tends to wear well among his intimates. In conversations, as in most cases, the popular "middle road" is best. That means being neither too silent nor too glib (油腔滑调的), and always knowing when to listen to others, but when to take your turn to carry the conversation.

- ***Not to Repeat***

Try not to repeat yourself, either by telling the same story again and again or by going back over details of your narrative that seemed especially interesting or amusing to your hearers. Avoid this as a habit, because an over dosage (剂量) of praise is like ten lumps of sugar in your coffee.

- ***Subjects to Be Avoided***

Certain subjects, even though you are very sure of the ground upon which you are standing, had best be shunned (避开) as the criticism of a religious creed or disagreement with another's age, income or salary, the prices of his or her possessions and so on.

The tactful person keeps his prejudices to himself. Even when he is involved in a discussion, if he finds other people's opinions unreasonable, he says, "Nothing of the kind!" then tries to find a more pleasant subject.

- ***Personal Remarks***

Although personal remarks are likely to be in bad form, it is proper and always pleasant to say something appreciative about something one has done. "Your speech was splendid!" "Such a delicious dinner you gave us." "I've never seen such beautiful flowers." and "You always know how to make a room inviting". But it is certain a bad taste to say "What a lovely nose you have!" or "Why don't you get married?"

2. *Communicative Skills*

As we all know, different cultures have different customary ways to express certain thoughts and emotions. Sometimes words with the same meaning produce different feelings in the listeners.

- ***Say the Polite Phrases***

"Thank you" is used much more frequently in the West than in China. When anyone does something for you, no matter how small and no matter whether he is a superior or waiter, it is proper to say "thank you". When something is offered to you, it is not polite to say, "I don't want it" as the Chinese manners would allow. You should say, "Yes, thank you" if you want it; or "No, thank you" if you refuse it.

"Beg your pardon" or "Excuse me" is often used in each of the following circumstances: if you accidentally knock or brush against someone; if you touch the arm or foot of someone sitting at table; if you are forced to pass in front of someone; if you find it necessary to interrupt a conversation; if you disturb someone at work, in reading, etc. you may say, "Pardon me," or "I beg your pardon, or "Excuse me". If it is a very small matter, the only reply necessary is a smile and a slight inclination of the head. Otherwise you may say "Certainly", or some reply suitable to the circumstances.

• ***Frankness and Directness***

Westerners tend to be frank and direct. Thus it is useful for a Chinese person to know the difference. Here are some additional cultural hints for your consideration, when you have conversations with them. First, if they want to criticize someone, they usually do it to his face, rather than use a third party to pass on the remarks. Similarly, if they receive criticism indirectly they are often very hurt. Second, when they want something they say "Yes" and when they don't they say "No, thanks". "No" here is not a polite refusal but a genuine "nothing to be needed". A host or hostess would no longer offer food or drink when the guests say "No". Third, people are expected to answer honestly when someone is asked a request. If they are not sure of doing something, they refuse directly without saying: "I'll try to do it." Finally, they don't consider "excessive modesty" a great virtue. When they receive compliments, they say "Thank you" rather than "Oh. No, you are flattering me."

• ***Personal Territory***

At home and in the office, desks and desk drawers are private territory. All things including stationeries, documents, journals or newspapers on the desk belong to the person whose desk it is, even if the desk itself is actually the state property. Nobody is allowed to pick them up without asking permission.

Children have their own bedroom. By the time they are teenagers they regard it as their own private territory. They may resent people entering without their permission. So it is common for even their father or mother to knock before going in.

• ***Privacy***

Like private territory, Westerners also have a strong sense of privacy. This concept develops round the personal interests and is often considered secrets, which are only shared with people very close to them. These touchy (难以处理的) topics include family life, marriage, religion, salary and political ideas and so on. So don't ask about or comment on their age and health unless they start the topic first. If they are asked questions that seem too personal to them, they would not answer them. Or they would just say: "Sorry, I don't know" or "I'm afraid that would be a strange question." They would also change the subject of conversation to something that is less personal.

Part Ⅶ Useful Words and Expressions

***Arriving and departing*:**

- Good morning / afternoon / evening.
- Fine, thank you.
- Good day Sir / Madam.
- Very well, thank you, and you?
- Hello (name), how are you?
- Not too bad.
- Hi / Hello! / What's up?
- So-so. / Can't complain.
- How are you doing?
- All right.
- How's everything?
- Good, thank you.
- How's it going?
- Fine / Great.
- It was a pleasure seeing you.
- See you (later).

***Inviting*:**

- I'd like ... to come to dinner with us.
- I hope you're not too busy to come.
- We sincerely hope you can attend the ceremony/ party/ meeting/ ball...
- May I have the honor of your company at cocktail party?
- The reception will be held in ... hotel, on...
- We have decided to have a get-together in honor of the occasion.

- The favor of a reply is requested.

Expressing thanks:

- How nice of you…
- How kind of you…
- How generous of you…
- How thoughtful of you
- I am so grateful to you for…
- How considerate of you…
- The gift will be a reminder of our friendship.
- The gift you sent is nice/ attractive/wonderful/great/pretty…
- … is highly appreciated by us.
- Thank you for inviting us to the wedding.

Introducing:

- This is (name).
- Pleased to meet you
- I'd like you to meet (name).
- It's a pleasure to meet you.
- I don't think you've met (name).
- Please allow me to introduce a friend of mine, (name).
- I've long heard about your name!
- (name), I'd like you to meet (name).
- I don't think you know (name).
- May I introduce you to (name).

Making a phone call:

- This is … speaking , may I speak to … ?
- I'll have him(or her) return your call as soon as possible.
- Would you mind holding the line, please?
- Just a moment please. / Hang on, please.
- Don't hang up, please.

- Would you mind giving your name please? I will take a message for you.
- He is in a conference. Can I get him to call you back?
- Could you ring again in 30 minutes, please?
- If you would like to hold the line for just a moment, I'll make some inquiries to see if I can get him.

Keys for Lead-in Exercises

1. 1)B 2)A 3)E 4)F 5)D 6)C
2. 1)C 2)B 3)A 4)C

Unit 2

The Etiquette of Behavior in Public Places

Part I Lead-in Exercises

1. ***Can you list some proper manners in public places?***

2. ***Please rank "Top Ten" from the following uncivilized conducts in campus life and compare them with your partners.***

1) Spit and litter at will.
2) Speak impolitely and scornfully.
3) Finish dining without putting a cutlery back.
4) Trample lawn, and pick flowers.
5) Paste up posters where they shouldn't come into view.
6) Leave the blackboard unclean before another class.
7) Play truant, absent without asking for a leave.
8) Smoke in the teaching area.
9) Cheat in an examination, and copy homework.
10) Scratch on the desks, walls, etc.
11) Damage public properties.
12) Waste food, water and electricity.
13) Take seats long before arriving.
14) Stay in the classroom without switching off mobile phone or turning it into silent mode.
15) Talk loudly in the library or classroom.
16) Read and spread unhealthy books and watch nasty video products.

17) Show excessive intimacy in public places.

18) Behave rudely in public places (such as picking nose, blowing one's nose, digging one's ears, sneezing at others).

19) Dress not properly in public places (such as dressing in slippers , a pajama and etc.).

20) Cut in lines or jump the queue (e. g. lunch time, shopping in supermarket).

Your answer: ______________________

3. ***Look at the following picture. Do you think they behave well or not? If not, Try to specify them.***

Part II Behavior Etiquette in Public Places

Nobody can stay away from the society and live alone. That means we have to set up a certain type of relationship with people around us wherever we are. So whether our behaviors are proper or not can definitely affect those around you. Proper behaviors may create a pleasant atmosphere while rude behaviors are likely to commit offences. A person who displays proper manners in public places not only feels good about himself; he also makes those around him feel respected and pleased.

The following principle of behavior etiquette in public places should be kept in minds.

1. *On the Buses*

Buses have been shuttling people from pillar to post for years. In all that time, the etiquette for riding on them has changed little and is still as relevant today as it was 100 years ago.

- Giving up your seat—Standing up for younger children especially those not yet in their teens is a matter of safety as they do not yet have as well defined a level of balance as an adult yet. It should go without saying that seats should be sacrificed for the elderly, the pregnant and the weak, too.
- Smells—If you're going to use buses (or any other form of public transport) you're going to be close to other users. Do them a favor and control excess smells; we're talking about body odour, bad breath and pungent food.
- Volume—Keep the volume down on your personal stereo! For heaven's sake, we don't want to hear it.
- Queues—Admittedly these days there are multiple queues for different buses all at the same stop. But try and remember who got there before when it comes to getting onto your bus and don't push too far ahead of others when your bus does eventually turn up accompanied by two others on the same route.
- Seating—Don't have a place for you and a place for your bag—you'll only have to put them on the floor when someone wants a seat. Also, don't sit on the aisle seat and leave the window seat vacant—it's just inconsiderate and unnecessary.

2. *In Library*

It seems that historically a library has been a place for research and studying. So it seems logical that these places be kept quiet for those doing research or studying. Some

people go to the library to study because it is quiet, maybe quieter than their homes. The people who want to talk also have rights, but they should be courteous to the people who would like a little quiet.

It no longer seems reasonable to expect that the library be absolutely silent, but when it starts to sound like a large party you know the volume has gone up a little too much. Moderation is key here. Many people dislike whispering but an equal number of people dislike hearing loud voices. If everyone is willing to compromise and use a quieter indoor voice then the people who want to talk may talk, and the people who want to study can do so productively.

3. *At the ATM / Bank*

Do not, ever, stand too close to someone who's using an ATM machine, unless they're close friends or lovers. If they're friends, but not close, you should wait by the deposit envelopes. If they're strangers, stay at least ten feet away and look distracted, though not obviously so, as in the case of a bad-actor-turned-burglar about to rob them.

Do not spend too much time at a single ATM; people are waiting and they have things to do. If you must treat the machine like your own personal accountant, spread your duties across multiple machines.

Getting into a bank, greeting from the bank teller should be responded with a polite reply. Ignoring someone is rude. If you want to dig through your purse for twenty minutes at the end of the transaction, do it somewhere where you're not tying up the entire line. Don't budge in line—if you walk in and see a big line, don't try to stand at the opposite end of the room and try to "dive in" and get to the teller before the next person in line. Expressions like "please", "thank you", "Excuse me" still do have a role in today's society.

4. *On the Street*

Your conduct on the street should always be modest and dignified. Ladies should carefully avoid all loud and boisterous conversation or laughter and all undue liveliness in public. In walking with a lady on the street give her the inner side of the walk, unless the outside if the safer part; in which case she is entitled to it.

As pedestrians on the pathway, we should all

pay heed to the following:

- Don't stroll along in the centre of the pavement, especially if holding hands with someone. Leave space for others walking faster to pass by.
- Don't go along reading a book or newspaper.
- If standing talking or at a bus stop, also leave space for passers-by.
- A keep-to-the-right (for some countries a keep-to-the-left) convention would be good to avoid those head-on encounters where both of you side-step.
- Please don't spit or discard chewing gum on the pavement.
- Don't swear or talk uproariously.
- Don't smoke or spit upon the walk, to the exceeding annoyance of those who are always disgusted with tobacco in any shape.
- Do not attract attention to yourself in public. This is one of the fundamental rules of good breeding.

5. *In a Restaurant*

Upon entering a restaurant, it's advisable to wait to be seated. The receptionist is always standing on the door to assist the guests to their preferred table. If by the next minute nobody bothered to acknowledge your presence, that's the time that you find a table.

"Cell phone or non-cell phone section?"

If you want to dine in a busy restaurant, get a reservation so that you could be seated on your preferred table. Specify your preference and be at the restaurant on time. It is rude not to arrive in a restaurant without calling your cancellation or delay. Remember that when you don't show up, the restaurant loses business for every minute of delay.

In calling for a waiter, always establish eye contact and raise your hand halfway to call his or her attention. In fine dining, eye contact is enough. In regular dining, you need a body gesture to get a waiter's attention. The waiter will appreciate it if you talk with them politely.

Let them greet you first before you ask for the menu. Once the menu is handed to you, take a look first. If not certain of the food that you are ordering, ask him for the restaurant's specialty or what food is often ordered there. When you are in a hurry, please specify a time. Do not tell the waiter to speed up the cooking after he leaves.

For details of dinning etiquette, refer to Unit Three.

6. *At Concert*

To be a good audience member it's important to know how to act in the theatre. It's quite different from watching television, going to a football game, or even going to the movies. Here are some tips explaining what is expected of audience members.

- ***Before you arrive*:**

Purchasing a ticket is required for a live theatre performance and it will be for a specific date and show. Be sure to check your ticket when you buy it, because tickets are not usually refundable or exchangeable.

Be on time. Often in a live performance, audience members will not be admitted if they arrive late, because they disturb the performance for the actors and other audience members. 15 minutes early will be appropriate.

Take care of personal needs (drinks of water, or restroom) because you won't be able to leave your seat until the intermission or until the performance ends. No food or drink is allowed in the theatre.

Depending on the type of performance you may want to make it special by dressing up for this special event. Opening night of a performance is always a dress-up night, and you may want to wear more formal clothes no matter when you attend. Try dressing up and you'll feel different!

- ***When you arrive*:**

An usher will usually greet you and ask for your ticket. With a general admission ticket, you get to pick your own seat. If your ticket has a row and seat number, the usher will check the number and show you to your assigned seat. Be sure to sit in the seat you are given so that you don't cause confusion for other audience members.

At most performances, you will receive a printed program. Get time to read it and find the names and information about people who are performing and helping to put on the show. It will make the show more enjoyable and you'll learn things that might surprise you.

• ***During the performance*:**

Listen! This is important because you will be hearing actors perform live for you. It's important that you listen very well so that you don't miss anything and so that you don't disturb others around you.

Respond! This is a live performance before a live audience. Your part is to let the actors know that you appreciate the show. Remember to always respond respectfully and appropriately. These are live actors and their performance will be affected by your reactions.

Be quiet and considerate of those around you! Don't kick the back of the seat in front of you, and don't talk during the performance, because it might disturb those around you.

• ***After the performance*:**

Applaud! When the performance is over, it's important to show your appreciation by applauding for the performers. In some performances, you might hear people applaud or cheer during the performance, and sometimes that's OK. But often the audience holds their applause until after the performance has ended. When you do applaud, respond enthusiastically.

Stay in your seat for the curtain call! At the end of the performance there is usually a curtain call. This is when the actors come on stage to receive your appreciation. Don't leave during the curtain call. Wait until it is over and then exit with the rest of the audience.

Stand and applaud if you really liked the show! Actors are thrilled when they receive something called a "Standing Ovation." If you want to pay them the highest praise, you might stand and applaud. It's reserved for the best performances! Hana Hou! Encore! At some musical performances you might hear audience members shouting "Hana Hou!" or "Encore!" This is another form of high praise and appreciation. The audience is asking the performer to please go on performing. In many cases, an entertainer will sing or play another song, making it a special performance.

7. *On the Subway Platform*

When entering the subway station pay utmost attention to the movements of the other travelers. Look for holes in the wave of those walking up the stairs and try to enter without disturbing the flow of human passage.

When your train arrives, always let passengers off the train before you get on. On occasion, you may find your train pulling into the station as you are still descending the stairs. In such a case, put spring into your step and attempt to get aboard. If you are successful: bravo. If you are unsuccessful: pay it no mind; you'll wait. If you're halfway in-between and are trying to wedge the doors open with your satchel: give it up. It's rude to the other passengers who are trying to reach their destination and the train conductor—a staunch proponent of urban etiquette—will never stand for it.

8. *In the Subway*

If riding alone, keep to yourself. Read your book, listen to music (whether portable or imagined), and stare at your feet. Don't engage other passengers in mild conversation; they're preoccupied with the same activities and usually don't wish to be disturbed. The very act of riding the subway is a performance in itself. While many riders may secretly wish to have a chat with you (you may be very hot), they are far too involved—as should you be—in complete submersion in their chosen character: that of the mute.

If riding with friends, you may, of course, speak freely with them. Keep conversation personal, quiet, and, whenever possible, not about any of the other passengers' appearance or fashion choices. In this case, keep to yourselves.

Subway trains are often crowded; if you're standing by a door as the train pulls into the station, and you're not getting off, get off anyway and allow people to exit the train, and then rush back in before the next wave starts moving.

Pregnant women, old people, the disabled, people with strollers, and children deserve seats more than you, unless you fall into one of those categories. You are under no obligation to give your seat away just because someone asks for it, but if they've gone so far as to ask, it's likely they need it more than you do.

9. *Use of Mobile Phones in Public Places*

There are some circumstances where a mobile phone should not be used at all. These are circumstances where the ringtone and ensuing conversation would be obtrusive, such as at a movie, concert, or church service. Ensure your mobile phone is off or on silent mode in these occasions.

There are some circumstances where using a mobile phone is fine, as long as the user does not imagine a phone booth around them, allowing them to shut out anyone who happens to be actually standing near them. Think of a person standing in line at the supermarket. Before she / he gets to the cash register, they may talk away freely. Once they get to the register, however, it's time to say "Look, I'll call you back in a minute" and hang up. Remember that the person standing behind the cash register is just that—a person, and should be treated as such.

And then there are some circumstances where using a mobile phone is fine, but it seems to irritate the rest of civilization, such as in a restaurant. If a person is sitting alone at a table, and the phone rings, and they talk at a normal (i. e not loud) volume, what's the problem? The only difference between this conversation and the one at the next table is that you can only see one of the people in this conversation.

As long as you don't ignore the people standing around you, and don't talk really loudly, and the conversation doesn't intrude on what you're doing, talk all you want.

Words and Expressions

shuttle	*n.* 往返汽车(列车、飞机)，航天飞机
odour	*n.* 气味，香味，臭味，意味，名声
aisle	*n.* 走廊，过道
courteous	*adj.* 有礼貌的，谦恭的

compromise	*n.* 妥协，折衷；*v.* 妥协，折衷，危及……的安全
from pillar to post	东奔西跑，到处碰壁
pungent	*adj.*（指气味、味道）刺激性的，辛辣的
boisterous	*adj.* 狂暴的，喧闹的
budge	*v.* 移动
stroll	*n.* 漫步，闲逛；*v.* 漫步，闲逛
pay heed to	注意，留意
uproariously	*adv.* 喧嚣地，吵闹地
usher	*n.* 引座员、引导；*v.* 引导，展示
standing ovation	*n.* 长时间起立鼓掌
encore	*n.* 再演唱的要求；*int.* 再演唱一次；*vt.* 要求再演或唱
bravo	*n.* 喝彩；*int.* 好啊！妙；*vt.* 喝彩
hedge	*n.* 楔 *v.* 楔入，挤入
satchel	*n.* 小背包
staunch	*adj.* 坚定的
obtrusive	*adj.* 鲁莽的，令人厌恶的，过分炫耀的
booth	*n.* 货摊，售货亭
intrude	*vi.* 闯入，侵入；*vt.* 强挤入，把（自己的思想）强加于人
scuff	*vi.* 拖足而行，磨损；*vt.* 以足擦地，践踏，使磨损
eccentric	*adj.* 古怪；*n.* 行为古怪的人

Part III Sample Dialogues

Sample Dialogue 1: At a Bank

Simon: Hi, Yang, do you know where the nearest bank is?

Yang: Er, let me see, opposite the main gate of our university there are two banks. I don't know what kind of card you use?

Simon: Just bank card, the West Bank. I wanna get some cash.

Yang: Right, I'll go with you to send some money to my cousin.

(At the West Bank.)

Simon: Oh, gee, look, so many people! We have to stand in a line.

Yang: Simon, follow me, we try the ATM outside.

(There are about three people at the ATM.)

Simon: Wait, Yang, wait, you can't jump the queue! We stand here.

Yang: Jump the queue? Sorry, I thought they were not in the line.

Simon: No, no, never stand too close to someone who's using an ATM machine, unless you're close friends or lovers. If a stranger, stay at least ten feet away.

Yang: Well, no wonder last time the old lady stared at me strangely. It seems we need to cultivate stronger sense in this aspect. Thank you, Simon.

Simon: Haa, welcome.

Sample Dialogue 2: At Concert

Nicola: Hurry, Yang, we will be late, just few minutes left.

Yang: Sorry, rush hour, you know rush hour. It took me more than half hour to arrive here.

Nicola: Oh, gee, why do you just put on a shirt?

Yang: I have no time to go back to dress more formally. You know, Prof. Michael's experiment is very difficult.

Nicola: Er, I have one more tie, come on, and put it on. The national orchestra will give us an electrifying performance of classic music.

Yang: Yeah, I've heard it before. It is said that the tickets were sold up three days ago.

Nicola: Right, almost every time like this.

Yang: Oh, I forgot to adjust my phone. Now change into vibration in case somebody calls me.

Nicola: Yes, me too, thanks, Yang, I'm too excited.

Sample Dialogue 3: On the Street

Yang: Sh, sh, keep silent; it's too late. Don't talk about the soccer loudly. Look, few people on the street, and we have to go back before 11 p. m, or my landlady will give me a sour face.

Jack: (lower voice) Yang, I know, but look over there.

Yang: Er, an old lady in front of us, I know. But she goes her way, and we go our way.

Jack: Now, listen! At night, if you're a man and you're walking along a street on which a woman is walking, and there are few people around, do not walk behind her.

Yang: Really? Is this also a kind of... etiquette?

Jack: And switch to the other side of the street and make a subtle noise—jingle change, half-whistle, but not wolf-whistle, scuff your shoes—so as to alert the female that a slightly eccentric but completely non-threatening male is within a hundred yards.

Yang: Oh, my god.

Jack: Exactly.

Yang: Er, you mean we should make some... noise?

Jack: Right, but not too loud.

Yang: We are young men, right? And we are young students, right?

Jack: Haa, yes, we sing a song.

Yang and Jack: *Pretty woman, walking down on the street, pretty woman...*

Sample Dialogue 4: In the Subway

Yang: So crowded, Christmas is coming, so many people go out for shopping.

Vera: Yes, Simon also went out for shopping. He wants to buy a blender to his mom.

Yang: Oh, I know. Vera, just now when I was in the train, I saw a very beautiful girl, so cool. I think she is also studying in our university.

Vera: Well, did you try to chat up?

Yang: Yeah, I tried, but no response.

Vera: What did you do?

Yang: Er, er, I said: You are also in Harvard? But she looked at me and said nothing.

Vera: Haa, does she have long hair?

Yang: En, yes, why?

Vera: I think she never heard you. She must listen to the iPod, like me. People who are in the train are usually preoccupied with the some activities such as listening to the MP3 or reading newspaper and usually don't wish to be disturbed.

Yang: My god, tell me earlier next time. Tomorrow I will ask her the same question when getting off the train.

Part IV Follow-up Practice

1. ***Place a check mark, or make a note, in the chart space underneath each type of performance to indicate whether the behavior in the first column is always OK, sometimes acceptable, or not acceptable.***

	Type of Event						
Behaviors	Sporting Event	Movie	Rock Concert	Orch Concert	Ballet	Opera	School Performance
Eating							
Talking							
Cheer during action or performance							

(Continued)

Type of Event							
Stand up or walk around during action or performance							
Give a standing ovation							
Applaud at end							
Clap along in time with music							

Discuss why it's OK to talk during some kinds of events, but not for others. Discuss special time to get up and walk around, such as intermission. If relevant, discuss special types of performance where behavior might be different from the usual, such as "participatory theater" performances.

2. ***Group work: Four students in a group make a discussion and list what are still regarded as rude behaviors besides those mentioned above. And then compare with another group.***

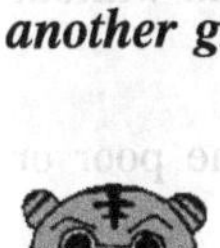

Part V Reading for Fun

Bank Etiquette

A rough old man walks into a bank and says to the teller at the window, "I want to open a damn checking account." The astonished woman replies, "I beg your pardon, sir. I must have misunderstood you. What did you say?"

"Listen up, damn it. I said I want to open a damn checking account right now!"

"I'm very sorry sir, but we do not tolerate that kind of language in this bank."

So saying, the teller leaves the window and goes over to the bank manager to tell him about her situation. They both return and the manager asks the old geezer, "What seems to be the problem here?"

"There's no damn problem," the man says, "I just won 50 million bucks in the damn lottery and I want to open a damn checking account in this damn bank!"

"I see," says the manager, "and this bitch is giving you a hard time?"

Part VI Supplementary Reading

Decencies of Behavior: To Who Wants to be a Gentleman

Do you want to be a gentleman? Read the following suggestions about what a gentleman should do or should not do, and see if you can become a real gentleman.

- A gentleman does not, and a man who aspires to be one must not, ever borrow money from a woman, nor should he, except in unexpected circumstances, borrow money from a man. Money borrowed without security is a debt of honor which must be paid without fail and promptly as possible.
- A gentleman never takes advantage of a woman in business dealing, nor of the poor or the helpless.
- One who is not well off does not "sponge (诈取别人钱财)," but pays his own way to the utmost of his ability.
- One who is rich does not make a display of his money or his possessions. Only a vulgarian (粗俗的富人) talks ceaselessly about how much this or that cost him.
- A very well-bred man intensely dislikes the mention of money, and never speaks of it (out of business hours) if he can avoid it.
- A gentleman never discusses his family affairs either in public or with acquaintances, nor does he speak more than casually about his wife.

- A man is a ungentlemanly man who tells anyone, no matter who, what his wife told him in confidence, or describes what she looks like in her bedroom. To impart details of her beauty is scarcely better than to publish her blemishes (污点,缺点); to do either is unspeakable.
- Nor does a gentleman ever criticize the behavior of a wife whose conduct is scandalous (诽谤性的). What he says to her in the privacy of their own apartments is no one's affair but his own, but he must never treat her with disrespect before their children, or a servant, or any one.
- A man of honor never seeks publicly to divorce his wife, no matter what he believes her conduct to have been; but for the protection of his own name, and that of the children, he allows her to get her freedom on other than criminal grounds. No matter who he may be, whether rich or poor, in high life or low, the man who publicly besmirches (抹上污点) his wife's name, besmirches still more his own, and proves that he is not, was not, and never will be, a gentleman.
- No gentleman goes to a lady's house if he is affected by alcohol. A gentleman seeing a young man who is not entirely himself in the presence of ladies, quietly induces the youth to depart. An older man addicted to the use of too much alcohol, need not be discussed, since he ceases to be asked to the houses of ladies.
- A gentleman does not lose control of his temper. In fact, in his own self-control under difficult or dangerous circumstances, lies his chief ascendancy over others who impulsively betray every emotion which animates them. Exhibitions of anger, fear, hatred, embarrassment, ardor or hilarity, are all bad form in public. And bad form is merely an action which "jars" the sensibilities of others. A gentleman does not show a letter written by a lady, unless perhaps to a very intimate friend if the letter is entirely impersonal and written by some one who is equally the friend of the one to whom it is shown. But the occasions when the letter of a woman may be shown properly by a man are so few that it is safest to make it a rule never to mention a woman's letter.
- A gentleman does not bow to a lady from a club window; nor according to good form should ladies ever be discussed in a man's club!
- The born gentleman avoids the mention of names exactly as he avoids the mention of what things cost; both are an abomination (憎恨,厌恶) to his soul.
- A gentleman's manners are an integral part of him and are the same whether in his dressing-room or in a ballroom, whether in talking to Mrs. Worldly or to the laundress bringing in his clothes. He whose manners are only put on in company is a veneered

(虚饰的) gentleman, not a real one.

- A man of breeding does not slap strangers on the back nor so much as lay his finger-tips on a lady. Nor does he punctuate (不时打断) his conversation by pushing or nudging (用肘轻推) or patting people, nor take his conversation out of the drawing-room! Notwithstanding the advertisements in the most dignified magazines, a discussion of underwear and toilet articles and their merit or their use, is unpleasant in polite conversation.
- All thoroughbred (受过良好教育的) people are considerate of the feelings of others no matter what the station of the others may be. Thackeray's climber who "licks the boots of those above him and kicks the faces of those below him on the social ladder" is a very good illustration of what a gentleman is *not*.
- A gentleman never takes advantage of another's helplessness or ignorance, and assumes that no gentleman will take advantage of him.

Part VII Useful Words and Expressions

Apologizing and forgiving:

- I am sorry for my carelessness.
- I am very sorry for being late. I was held up by the traffic jam.
- Sorry to make you upset.
- Sorry to cause the inconvenience to you.
- I am sorry to have given you so much trouble.
- I am sorry to have taken up so much your time.
- I've got a bit of an apology to make, you see…
- I'm afraid I've got something to tell you.
- Oh, that's alright, don't worry.
- It's not really your fault.
- Please don't blame yourself.
- Oh, never mind, it doesn't really matter.

Asking for permission:

- May I have permission to smoke here?
- May I take your newspaper to read on bus. There is something I am really interested in.
- I wonder if you could permit me to take this book back home for two days.
- Do you mind if I take this seat?
- I wonder if I could possibly use your car.
- Yes, go ahead.
- Oh, well, all right.
- No, I wouldn't mind.
- As you wish.
- I'd rather you didn't.
- I'm sorry. I will use it tomorrow.

Offering help:

- Is there anything I can do for you?
- Can I give you a hand?
- Do you need some assistance?
- May I help you?
- It seems as if you needed a hand. Let me help you.
- Yes, please. If you wouldn't mind.
- It's kind of you. Thanks.
- No, don't bother. I can do it myself.
- No, it's all right. I can mange.

Making a booking:

- I'd like to reserve a single room from Setp. 1 to Setp 5.
- I'd like to book two tickets for Friday's performance.
- Could you make arrangements for a dinner party for ten tomorrow evening?
- We do have single room available for these dates.
- There are two performances on Friday. The Matrtinee at three o'clock in the afternoon, and the evening performance at 8 o'clock in the evening. Which performance do you like?

Unit 3

The Etiquette of Dining

Part I Lead-in Exercises

1. ***Have you ever tried Western-style dish? If yes, tell your partner how you feel about it. If no, imagine what it is like according to the knowledge you've got.***

2. ***Vocabulary building: Match the Chinese words on the left column with their appropriate English expressions on the right.***

1)欧式西餐	A. buffet
2)餐巾	B. dressing
3)招牌菜	C. flatware
4)餐具	D. appetizer
5)甜食	E. serving spoon
6)沙拉调味汁	F. napkin
7)开胃菜	G. desserts
8)公用匙	H. Continental cuisine
9)自助餐	I. specialty
10)托盘	J. saucer

1)________ 2)________ 3)________ 4)________ 5)________

6)________ 7)________ 8)________ 9)________ 10)________

Part II Table Etiquette and Manners

Table manners have always played an important part in making a favorable impression. Our actions at the table and while eating can be essential to how others perceive us and can even affect our professional success.

Many Chinese who go to a formal Western dinner for the first time may be surprised by such different table etiquette and manners in Western culture. Knowing some basics may help you make a good impression. The idea is that if there are standards that people abide by, then you can have confidence that you are behaving "appropriately". In this part you are going to know some basics about Table Etiquette and Manners.

1. *Table Setting*

Table setting is of great importance for western-style dish, especially for formal occasions. The table should have a centerpiece that performs a solely decorative function. If an informal dinner is being served that will fill the available places at the table, care should be taken to not make the centerpiece too large so that there will be sufficient room to place serving dishes. However, at a formal dinner, the centerpiece may be huge and, including candles, may extend the full length of the table. Centerpieces should be of low height, so as not to obstruct visibility of diners' faces.

Informal settings generally have fewer utensils and dishes but use a stereotyped layout based on more formal settings. Utensils are arranged in the order and the way a person will use them. Usually in Western culture, that means that the forks, bread plate, spreader, and napkin are to the left, while knives, spoons, drinkware, cups, and saucers are to the right, although the left-right order is reversed in a minority of countries.

Informal table setting

Formal table setting

1. butter knife
2. bread-and-butter plate
3. soup spoon
4. seafood fork
5. seafood knife
6. meat and salad fork
7. dinner knife
8. decoration plate
9. Soup bowl
10. dessert spoon
11. dessert fork
12. water glass
13. Champagne glass
14. Wine glass (for red)
15. wineglass (for white)

Utensils are placed about one inch from the edge of the table, each one lining up at the base with the one next to it. Utensils on the outermost position are used first (for example, a salad fork and a soup spoon, then the dinner fork and the dinner knife). The blade of the knife must face toward the plate. The glasses are positioned about an inch from the knives, also in the order of use: white wine, red wine, dessert wine, and water tumbler.

Should you be attending a formal dinner or banquet with pre-set place settings, it is possible to gain clues about what may be served by "reading" the place setting. Start by drawing an imaginary line through the center of the serving plate (the plate will be placed in the center of your dining space). To the right of this imaginary line all of the following will be placed; glassware, cup and saucer, knives, and spoons, as well as a seafood fork if the meal includes seafood. It is important to place the glassware or cup back in the same position after its use in order to maintain the visual presence of the table. To the left of this imaginary line all of the following will be placed; bread and butter plate (including small butter knife placed horizontally across the top of the plate), salad plate, napkin, and forks. Remembering the rule of "liquids on your right" and "solids on your left" will help in allowing you to quickly become familiar with the place setting.

2. *Napkin Use*

The meal begins when the host unfolds his or her napkin. This is your signal to do the same. Place your napkin on your lap, completely unfolded if it is a small luncheon napkin or in half, lengthwise, if it is a large dinner napkin. Typically, you want to put your napkin on your lap soon after sitting down at the table (but follow your host's lead).

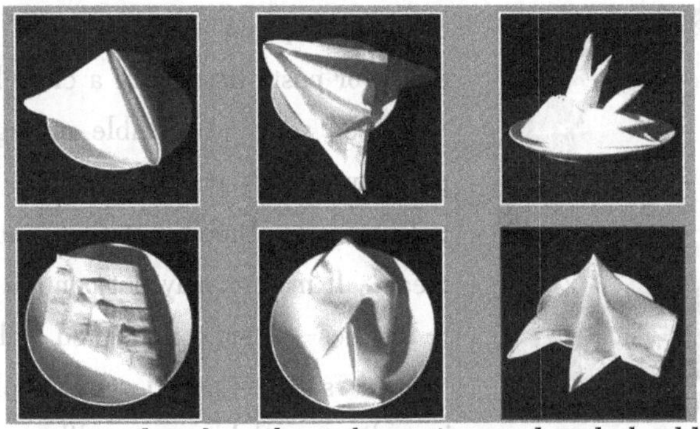

The napkin remains on your lap throughout the entire meal and should be used to gently blot your mouth when needed. If you need to leave the table during the meal, place your napkin on your chair as a signal to your server that you will be returning. The host will signal the end of the meal by placing his or her napkin on the table. Once the meal is over, you too should place your napkin neatly on the table to the right of your dinner plate.

3. *Ordering Food*

It may be a little puzzling for the Chinese to understand the menu in a western-style restaurant and get to know where to start. Some general knowledge may offer you some help.

"Steak? Let's go with the fish. It's brain food. After, if you still think eating steak is a good idea, we'll do that."

When the waiter or waitress comes with a menu, you may start your food ordering. If you are a guest at a meal, ask the person what he/she recommends. By doing this, you will learn price range guidelines and have an idea of what to order. Usually order an item in the mid price range.

Generally there are six or seven types of dish on menu for western-style dish.

- Appetizer: It is a type of small snack before a meal. Because it aims to make people have good appetite, it is of special flavor, small in quantity and high in quality. It mainly tastes salty and sour. For example, stewed sausage with cream, fried herring with egg sauce.
- Soup: Different from Chinese dish, the second course of western-style dish is soup. Here are some soup types:

Potato leek soup

—Clear soup—A combination of vegetables, meat, grains or pasta floating in a clear broth or stock.

—Pureed soup—Vegetable or legume soups either partially or fully pureed.

—Chowders—Diced potatoes and broth, milk or cream. It may or may not contain fish or seafood.

—Bisques—A soup thickened with rice or roux.

—Cold soup—Cooked and cooled or uncooked ingredients. Cold soups, like cold food, require more seasoning than hot.

- Side dish: Usually, fish-dish will be taken as the third course, also called side dish, including river and sea fish and etc. Because this type of food is easy to digest, it often goes before the main course.
- Main course: Its main materials are beef, mutton and pork. Roast, fry and grill are the main ways to cook the main course.

Beef steak

Codfish steak

- Vegetable dish: It can be either offered after the main course or with the main course. Vegetable dish is usually called salad, made from lettuce, tomato, cucumber and etc. The main condiment is called "dressing".
- Dessert: Actually, all food after the main course can be taken as the sixth dish, including pudding, cakes, ice cream, cheese, fruit and etc.
- Drinks: Coffee and tea will be offered as the last dish.

Usually what you need to decide first is main course. You don't need to order seven types unless you have a very good appetite and a big stomach. It is impolite to order a lot, but not finish all. It will be the good choice to order the main course, appetizer, soup and

Desserts

dessert, if it is enough. Of course, you can also order something you prefer most.

4. *Use of Silverware*

Choosing the correct silverware from the variety in front of you is not as difficult as it may first appear. Starting with the knife, fork, or spoon that is farthest from your plate, work your way in, using one utensil for each course. The salad fork is on your outermost left, followed by your dinner fork. Your soupspoon is on your outermost right, followed by your beverage spoon, salad knife and dinner knife. Your dessert spoon and fork are above your plate or brought out with dessert. If you remember the rule to work from the outside in, you'll be fine.

There are two ways to use a knife and fork to cut and eat your food. They are the American style and the European or Continental style. Either style is considered appropriate. In the American style, one cuts the food by holding the knife in the right hand and the fork in the left hand with the fork tines piercing the food to secure it on the plate. Cut a few bite-size pieces of food, then lay your knife across the top edge of your plate with the sharp edge of the blade facing in. Change your fork from your left to your right hand to eat, fork tines facing up. (If you are left-handed, keep your fork in your left hand, tines facing up.) The European or Continental style is the same as the American style in that you cut your meat by holding your knife in your right hand while securing your food with your fork in your left hand. The difference is your fork remains in your left hand, tines facing down, and the knife in your right hand. Simply eat the cut pieces of food by picking them up with your fork still in your left hand.

5. *Meals Finished*

Do not push your plate away from you when you have finished eating. Leave your plate where it is in the place setting. The common way to show that you have finished your meal is to lay your fork and knife diagonally across your plate. Place your knife and fork side by side, with the sharp side of the knife blade facing inward and the fork, tines down, to the left of the knife. Make sure they are placed in such a way that they do not slide off the plate as it is being removed. Once you have used a piece of silverware, never place it back on the table. Do not leave a used spoon in a cup, either; place it on the saucer. You can leave a soupspoon in a soup plate. Any unused silverware is simply left on the table.

6. *Food to Eat with Fingers*

- Bacon: When bacon is cooked until it is very crisp, and there is no danger of getting the fingers wet with grease, it is okay to pick it up to eat it. This is an instance of practicality winning out over decorum, since trying to cut a crisp piece of bacon usually results in crushing it into shards that are quite difficult to round up onto a fork.
- Bread: Bread must always be broken, never cut with a knife. Tear off a piece that is no bigger than two bites worth and eat that before tearing off another. If butter is provided (and at formal events it customarily is not), butter the small piece just before eating it. There is an exception to this rule: if you are served a hot roll, it is permissible to tear (not cut) the whole roll lengthwise down the middle and place a pat of butter inside to melt.
- Cookies: It is never necessary to try to eat the cookie that comes as a garnish to your dessert with a spoon. Unless it has fallen so far into the chocolate sauce that there isn't a clean corner by which to pick it up.
- Chips, French Fries, Fried Chicken, and Hamburgers: All these items (which could also probably be classified as "fast foods") simply will not be served in a formal setting. Most are intended to be eaten with the hands, although a particularly messy hamburger could be approached with fork and knife, and steak fries (the thick-cut, less crispy variety) may be best eaten with a fork.
- Small Fruits and Berries on the Stem: If you are served strawberries with the hulls on,

cherries with stems, or grapes in bunches, then it is okay to eat them with your fingers. Otherwise, as with all berries, the utensil of choice is a spoon. In the case of grapes, you may encounter a special scissors, to be used to cut off a small cluster from the bunch. If not, tear a portion from the whole, rather than plucking off single grapes, which leaves a cluster of unattractive bare stems on the serving platter.

7. *General Table Manners*

- Chew with your mouth closed.
- Do not talk at an excessively loud volume and do not make loud or unusual noises while eating.
- Refrain from burping, coughing, sneezing or blowing nose at the table. If you must do so, you may request that your action be excused.
- Never tilt back your chair while at the table. Sit in a relaxed and comfortable position, but do not "slouch".
- Always ask the host or hostess to be excused before leaving the table.
- Do not stare at anyone while he or she is eating. It is considered rude.
- Never talk on your phone or text a friend at the table. If an urgent matter arises, ask host or hostess to be excused, and step away from the table.

Works and Expressions

abide by	遵守……;依从……
stereotyped	*adj.* 老一套的;缺少新奇和创造力的
obstruct	*v.* 阻隔,阻塞
utensils	*n.* 器具
outermost	*adj.* 最外面的, 最远的
luncheon	*n.* 午晏、正式的午餐
blot	*n.* 污渍, 污点; *v.* 弄污
stew	*v.* 炖, 焖, 受闷热
herring	*n.* 青鱼, 鲱
broth	*n.* 肉汤

(Continued)

chowders	*n.* 杂烩汤:一种同这种海鲜汤相似的汤
pasta	*n.* 意大利面制品，意大利面食(包括通心粉及面条等)
dice	*vt.* 切成方块
bisque	*n.* (乳脂,番茄等的)浓汤,桔黄色的
roux	*n.* roux (Fr.)掺油面粉糊(用于做浓羹汤)
ingredient	*n.* 成分，因素
seasoning	*n.* 调味品，调料
beef	*n.* 牛肉
mutton	*n.* 羊肉
grill	*n.* 烤架，铁格子，烤肉; *v.* 烧，烤
lettuce	*n.* 生菜
condiment	*n.* 调味品
silverware	*n.* 银餐具
tine	*n.* 尖头，尖，齿，叉
diagonally	*adv.* 对角地
crisp	*adj.* 脆的，易碎的
grease	*n.* 油脂
garnish	*v.* 装饰
hull	*n.* (果实等的)外壳
cluster	*n.* 串，丛; *vi.* 丛生，成群
platter	*n.* 大浅盘
burp	*v.* 打饱嗝
slouch	*v.* 懒散

Part III Sample Dialogues

Sample dialogue 1: Restaurant Reservation

Waiter: Princess Restaurant. Good morning! Can I help you?

Caller: Yes, I would like to book a table for four for the next Wednesday, December 23.

Waiter: Certainly, sir. What time do you like your table?

Caller: At 8:30 on next Wednesday evening.

Waiter: May I have your name, sir, please?

Caller: Please book it under the name of Mr. Watson.

Waiter: So it's Mr. Watson, a table for four for the evening of the next Wednesday. It is Western food and you are coming at 8:30.

Caller: That's right.

Waiter: Thank you for calling us. We look forward to your visit.

Sample dialogue 2: Ordering Food

(Waiter = W   Mr. Green = Mr   Mrs. Green = Mrs)

(8:00 p. m. at the restaurant)

W: Here's the menu for this evening. I'll come and take your order when you're ready.

Mrs: What soup would you like to have, dear?

Mr: I'd like to have country soup this evening.

Mrs: Ok. But I prefer creamed mushroom soup here.

W: Can I take your order now?

Mrs: A country soup and a creamed mushroom soup. And... a fish steak for me.

Mr: I'll have a beef steak.

W: Would you like the steak well done or rare?

Mr: I'd like it medium.

W: Mediufm beef steak... And what else would you like to have?

Mrs: Vanilla (香草) ice-cream for me.

Mr: Ah, I want carrots and string beans. French dressing on the salad, please.

W: Very good, sir. Would you care for something to drink?

Mr: Yes, a glass of orange juice and a pint of beer.

Sample dialogue 3: *Serving Dishes*

A: Here is the fried beef with green pepper and onion.

B: Mm, It looks good. And I have ordered another dish-plain fried shrimps.

A: It's coming.

B: What is this?

A: It's sweet and sour pork.

B: I'm afraid there is a mistake. I ordered a sweet and sour fish.

A: I'm sorry, sir. I got it wrong. Will you keep the sweet and sour pork, or should I get the sweet and sour fish for you?

B: That's all right. I'll take it anyway.

A: Thank you very much.

Sample dialogue 4: *Ways of Paying*

(Waiter = W   Mr. Bell(B) = B   Mrs. Bell(M) = M)

(The Bells are paying for their dinner.)

W: (When he sees Mr. Bell wave to him, he comes over.) Would you like anything else, sir and madam?

B: No, thank you. We'll take the check now.

W: Yes, sir. (Gives the check to Mr Bell) Here it is, sir.

B: (Goes over the bill) What's the 21 dollars for?

W: For the three coffees.

M: We only had two!

W: (Checks the bill carefully) Oh, I'm awfully sorry, madam.

(The waiter goes back to the cashier to have the amount changed.)

W: I'm sorry to have kept you waiting. Would you mind checking it again?

B: That's all right.

W: Would you please sign for it, sir?

B: Yes, thank you.

Part IV Follow-up Practice

1. ***We' ve learnt a lot about western-style dish. What are the differences between Chinese-style dish and Western-style dish? Try to list some.***

2. ***Since we've goe Sonce information about table setting, find out what the following items are named and fill into the blanks of the table.***

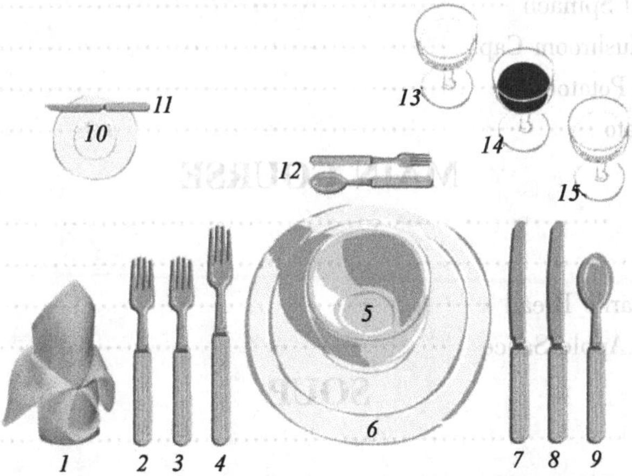

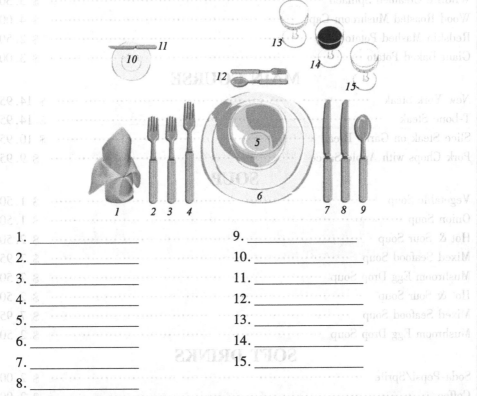

1. ______________
2. ______________
3. ______________
4. ______________
5. ______________
6. ______________
7. ______________
8. ______________
9. ______________
10. ______________
11. ______________
12. ______________
13. ______________
14. ______________
15. ______________

3. ***Role play: Lin Ping is an oversea student in USA. He gets into a restaurant and the waiter comes to greet him. Design a dialogue for them. You may refer to some useful expressions in sample dialogues.***

4. ***You are inviting your American friend to dinner. Now let's look at the menu of a***

restaurant and try to use it to practice a short dialogue about ordering food.

Dinner Menu

STARTERS

Baked French Onion Soup	$ 2.95
Grilled Chicken and Portobello Mushroom Skewers	$ 7.50
Stewed sausage with cream	$ 5.00

POTATOES AND VEGETABLES

Wildfire Creamed Spinach	$ 3.50
Wood Roasted Mushroom Caps	$ 4.00
Redskin Mashed Potatoes	$ 2.50
Giant Baked Potato	$ 3.00

MAIN COURSE

New York Steak	$ 14.95
T-bone Steak	$ 14.95
Slice Steak on Garlic Bread	$ 10.95
Pork Chops with Apple Sauce	$ 9.95

SOUP

Vegetable Soup	$ 1.50
Onion Soup	$ 1.50
Hot & Sour Soup	$ 2.50
Mixed Seafood Soup	$ 7.95
Mushroom Egg Drop Soup	$ 2.50
Hot & Sour Soup	$ 2.50
Mixed Seafood Soup	$ 7.95
Mushroom Egg Drop Soup	$ 2.50

SOFT DRINKS

Soda-Pepsi/Sprite	$ 2.00
Coffee	$ 2.00
Milk	$ 2.00
Tea	$ 2.00
Iced Tea	$ 2.00
Juice-Orange/ Apple	$ 2.25

Part V Reading for Fun

Spoon

Fella goes into his favorite deli(熟食店) where the waiter immediately brings him a bowl of matzo(未发酵的面包) ball soup. The customer signals the waiter to come back.

"Taste the soup!" he commands.

"Why?" inquires the surprised waiter.

"Taste the soup!" comes the reply.

"Max, you've been coming in here every day for ten years. There's never been anything wrong with the soup."

"Taste the soup!"

"What's wrong, too much salt—not enough salt?"

"Taste the soup!"

"What, the matzo balls aren't soft enough for you?"

"TASTE THE SOUP!"

The waiter finally agrees, "All right all right, I'll taste the soup! Where's the spoon?"

"A-HA!" chortles(咯咯地笑) Max.

Part VI Supplementary Reading

Tips and Pitfalls

1. *Beginning*

Developing the habit of taking a moment to observe which starting method will be operative at an event can be very useful in preventing awkward mistakes. It will ensure, for example, that an agnostic(不明朗的) guest never finds himself with laden(装满的) fork pushed halfway into his mouth just as the host begins to say grace(做饭前祷告).

There are two common approaches to determining how to begin, and, whichever method is used, it should be followed at the start of each course of the meal. At smaller events, it is common to wait to take a bite until everyone at the table has received a serving and the hostess has begun eating. Sometimes a hostess may urge her guests to eat immediately upon receiving the food. This is especially true at larger events, where waiting for everyone would allow it to get cold. In this case, wait until one or two of the other guests are ready to begin as well, so that you are not the only person at the table who is eating.

2. *Posture*

"Elbows, elbows, if you're able—keep your elbows off the table!"

Proper posture at the table is very important. Sit up straight, with your arms held near your body. You should neither lean on the back of the chair nor bend forward to place the elbows on the table. It is permissible to lean forward slightly every now and then and press the elbows very lightly against the edge of the table, if it is obvious that you are not using them for support.

3. *Eating Soup*

Dip the spoon into the soup, moving it away from the body, until it is about two-thirds full, then sip the liquid (without slurping) from the side of the spoon (without inserting the whole bowl of the spoon into the mouth). The theory behind this is that a diner who scoops(舀,盛) the spoon toward himself is more likely to slosh(溅、波) soup onto his lap, although it is difficult to imagine what sort of eater would stroke the spoon so forcefully through the liquid that he creates waves. It is perfectly fine to tilt the bowl slightly—again away from the body—to get the last spoonful or two of soup.

4. *Finger Bowls*

The finger bowl has been on the brink(濒于) of obsolescence (荒废, 退化) for over a century without entirely disappearing. This is probably why it provides the critical obstacle in the story of the man, either a foreigner or a bumpkin(土包子, 乡巴佬), who is a guest at a formal dinner party. When a servant offers him a bowl of water at the end of the meal, he drinks it. The hostess presiding(主持, 负责) at the event is so poised(泰然自若的) and utterly well-mannered that, without hesitation, she drinks her bowl down, too, thus saving him the embarrassment of realizing the extent of his faux pas. This tale has reached almost the status of urban legend, and it is told in many variations(变化).

The hostess may be a family matriarch(高雅的老妇人) or someone very well-known, say Eleanor Roosevelt or Queen Victoria, but the finger bowl seems to be a constant.

Fortunately, the main difficulty lies in recognizing the finger bowl when you see it, which, at formal events, will be either before or after the dessert course. Often there is a slice(优美地,微妙地)of lemon floating in the water. Once you are presented with one, all you need to know is that you should delicately dip your fingertips in the water (no scrubbing 洗擦), dry them off with your napkin (equally delicately), and set the bowl to the side of your plate.

5. *Removing Inedible Items from the Mouth*

The general rule for removing food from your mouth is that it should go out the same way it went in. Therefore, olive pits can be delicately dropped onto an open palm before putting them onto your plate, and a piece of bone discovered in a bite of chicken should be returned to the plate by way of the fork. Fish is an exception to the rule. It is fine to remove the tiny bones with your fingers, since they would be difficult to drop from your mouth onto the fork. And, of course, if what you have to spit out will be terrifically ugly—an extremely fatty piece of meat that you simply can't bring yourself to swallow, for example—it will be necessary to surreptitiously(秘密地)spit it into your napkin, so that you can keep it out of sight.

Table Manners in China from the Eyes of a Foreigner

Of course, the main difference on the Chinese dinner table is chopsticks instead of knife and fork, but that's only superficial. Besides, in decent restaurants, you can always ask for a pair of knife and fork, if you find the chopsticks not helpful enough. The real difference is that in the West, you have your own plate of food, while in China the dishes are placed on the table and everyone shares. If you are being treated to a formal dinner and particularly if the host thinks you're in the country for the first time, he will do the best to give you a taste of many different types of dishes.

The meal usually begins with a set of at least four cold dishes, to be followed by the main courses of hot meat and vegetable dishes. Soup then will be served (unless in Guangdong style restaurants) to be followed by staple food ranging from rice, noodles to dumplings. If you wish to have your rice to go with other dishes, you should say so in good time, for most of the Chinese choose to have the staple food (主食) at last or have none of them at all.

Perhaps one of the things that surprises a Western visitor most is that some of the Chinese hosts like to put food into the plates of their guests. In formal dinners, there are always "public" chopsticks and spoons for this purpose, but some hosts may use their own chopsticks. This is a sign of genuine friendship and politeness. It is always polite to eat the food. If you do not eat it, just leave the food in the plate.

People in China tend to over-order food, for they will find it embarrassing if all the food is consumed. When you have had enough, just say so. Or you will always overeat!

Part VII Useful Words and Expressions

Cooking Method	Condiments
fried… 煎……	table salt 食盐
deep fried… 炸(干炸)……	sugar 白糖
quick-fried/stir-fried… (爆)炒……	cheese 奶酪/干酪
braised… 炖(烧)……	vinegar 醋
stewed… 闷(炖、煨)……	butter 黄油
steamed… 蒸……	pepper 胡椒
smoked… 熏……	soy sauce 酱油
roast… 烤……	cream 奶油
grilled… 烤……	curry 咖哩
crisp… 香酥……	mustard 芥末
spicy… 麻辣……	tomato sauce 番茄酱
mashed… ……馅泥……	honey 蜂蜜
in brown sauce 红烧	gravy 肉汁
in soy sauce 酱汁……	jam 果酱
in hot sauce 干烧……	cube sugar 方糖
in tomato sauce 茄汁……	ginger 姜
with fish flavor 鱼香……	garlic 大蒜
with sweet and sour flavor 糖醋……	shallot 大葱
shreds… ……丝	mayonnaise 蛋黄酱
slices… 片……	sweet soybean paste 甜面酱
cubes… ……块	

Western Entrees	Dessert
beef steak　牛排 (rare)　半熟的(牛排) roast beef　烤牛排 medium-rare　适中偏生的(牛排) curry beef　咖哩牛排 real cutlet/veal chop　小牛排 roast veal　烤小牛排 (well done)　熟透的(牛排) spiced beef　五香牛排 braised beef　焖牛排 roast mutton　烤羊肉 lamb chop　羊排 pork chop　猪排 sliced ham　火腿片 roast turkey　烤火鸡 roast chicken　烤油鸡 curried chicken　咖哩鸡 roast duck　烤鸭 fried fish　炸鱼 fried eggs　煎鸡蛋 boiled eggs　煮鸡蛋 poached eggs　荷包蛋 omelet/omelette　摊鸡蛋/蛋卷 pickled cucumber　酸黄瓜 salad　色拉 salad dressing　色拉酱 chicken salad　鸡色拉 vegetable salad　素菜色拉 ham salad　火腿色拉 baked potato　烤土豆 mashed potato　土豆泥	cake　蛋糕 cream cake　奶油蛋糕 ice-cream　冰淇淋 pie　馅饼 vanilla ice-cream　香草冰淇淋 shortcake　松饼 chocolate ice-cream　巧克力冰淇淋 tart　果馅饼 strawberry ice-cream　草霉冰淇淋 apple pie　苹果馅饼 ice sucker　冰棍 jello　冰糕 pastry　点心 yam　甜薯 sweet potato　番薯 raisin　葡萄干 **Drinks** coffee　咖啡 black coffee　不加牛奶的咖啡/清咖啡 white coffee　牛奶咖啡 coffee with cream and sugar　加奶加糖的咖啡 instant coffee　速溶咖啡 green tea　绿茶 black tea　红茶 jasmine tea　茉莉花茶 tea bags　袋泡茶 yogurt　酸奶 fruit juice　水果汁 mineral water　矿泉水 soda water　汽水 fresh orange juice　鲜桔子汁 beer　啤酒 light beer　淡啤酒

- I want to make a reservation for three people for this evening at 6:30.
- I'd like to reserve a table for tomorrow evening at 7 o'clock. It's for five. I'd like a non-smoking section.
- Are you ready to order? /May I take your order?
- We'd like some specialties. Can you recommend some?
- What would you like to drink?
- I also like a chef's salad.
- What would you like for dessert?
- I'd like something typically French.
- Let's go Dutch.
- It's my treat today.

Keys for Lead-in exercises

1)H 2)F 3)I 4)C 5)G 6)B 7)D 8)E 9)A 10)J

Follow-up practice 2

1. napkin
2. Salad fork
3. Seafood fork
4. Dinner fork
5. Soup bowl
6. Flatware
7. Dinner knife
8. Seafood knife
9. Soup spoon
10. Bread-and-butter plate
11. Butter knife
12. Dessert spoon and fork
13. Champagne glass
14. Wine glass (for red)
15. Wine glass (for white)

Unit 4

The Etiquette of Dressing

Part I Lead-in Exercises

1. ***Please match the specific wear on the left side with the dress codes on the right side respectively.***

1) T-shirt and jeans	A. White Tie.
2) Tailcoat	B. Black Tie.
3) Tuxedo	C. Formal business attire.
4) Polo shirt	D. Business casual
5) Suit	E. Casual wear

2. ***Discuss with your classmates why jeans are so popular among young people throughout the world.***

3. ***What do you think you should be dressed on the following occasions. Discuss with your partners.***

- At an evening party held by the British Embassy.
- At your friend's birthday party.
- At office.
- In a professor's home.
- At sports meeting.
- At a job interview.
- At concert.
- In a stadium to watch football game.

Part II The Etiquette of Dressing

Clothes to us are similar to what fur and feathers to beasts and birds; yet they not only keep us warm and decent, but they also show the social etiquette. The way you dress yourself in a social or business environment can reveal a lot about you and your life and it also may contribute a lot to how others think of you.

Successful dressing doesn't necessarily mean wearing something expensive and splendid, but following the TPO norm, which is the initials of time, place and occasion respectively. It means having you dressed fit to different time, place and occasion.

1. *Formal wear*

Many formal social events have specific dress codes, each of which calls for particular kinds of dress for both women and men. Formal wear is a general term used to describe clothing suitable for formal events. Western formal wear has had a pervasive influence on styles in many countries.

Let's get to know the two most formal dress codes. Both of them are evening wear, worn only after six o'clock in the evening, or after sundown during winter months. One is formal evening wear, also known as full dress or white tie, the other is semiformal evening wear, or black tie.

What type of formal attire is expected for special events and formal affairs, one may get the clue from invitations. We will take men's attire as examples, women wear their counterparts respectively.

If the invitation reads "White Tie" or "Full Dress", the ultimate in formal dress is required and a strict attention to tradition should be paid. Generally speaking, the guest is not permitted to deviate from an accepted standard.

Component elements of white tie for men:

- Tailcoat
- Formal trousers, (with satin stripes on the left and right sides) which are never cuffed
- White pique bow tie
- White (black on some occasions) pique vest
- White pique-front shirt
- Cuff links and studs
- Black patent leather shoes
- Suspenders may also be worn

White tie

Component elements of white tie for women:

- Ball gown—ballerina (to the ankle) or full-length (to the floor)
- Dancing shoes—formal pumps or sandal shoes
- Jewellery—earrings and necklace; rings and bracelets are optional
- Gloves—if they are worn, should be opera length (evening gloves or opera gloves are a type of formal glove that reaches beyond the elbow)
- Stole or cloak
- Handbag—clutch style or small evening bag

White tie is seldom called for in one's life, since it is a dress code for ultra-formal occasions such as prize-offering party or royal dinner.

Usually, tuxedo is highly advised in the following circumstances: invites stating black tie or formal; opening of symphony, ballet or opera; formal dance; private and public formal reception or party; formal restaurant dining. If the invitation reads "Black Tie", it requires you to dress formally. Black tie' s daytime equivalents are morning dress for formal daytime events.

Ball gown

Component elements of black tie for men:

- Tuxedo or dinner jacket
- Formal trousers
- Formal shirt, which may have a wing collar and may have a pleated, standard, or pique front (or may have a ruffled front)

Formal pumps

Opera gloves

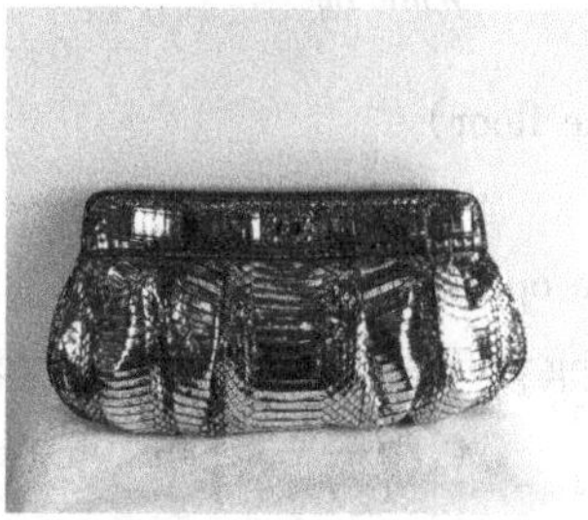

Handbag-clutch style

Stole

- A bow tie or neck tie
- A waistcoat or vest (worn with either a bow tie or a long tie)

- Black patent leather shoes
- Cufflinks and studs
- Suspenders may also be worn

Component elements of black tie for women:

- Cocktail dresses or dressy evening separates
- Dressy jewellery

If the invitation says "Black Tie Preferred", it shows that the host prefers guests to wear formal evening attire to the special occasion. Black Tuxedo, White Tie Dinner Jacket or a dark contemporary style tuxedo are acceptable (no Tailcoats). Non-formal Dress Suits are also acceptable, but not preferred.

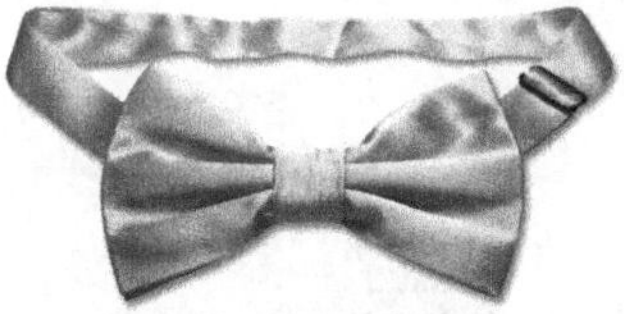

Bow tie

Neck tie

Cufflinks

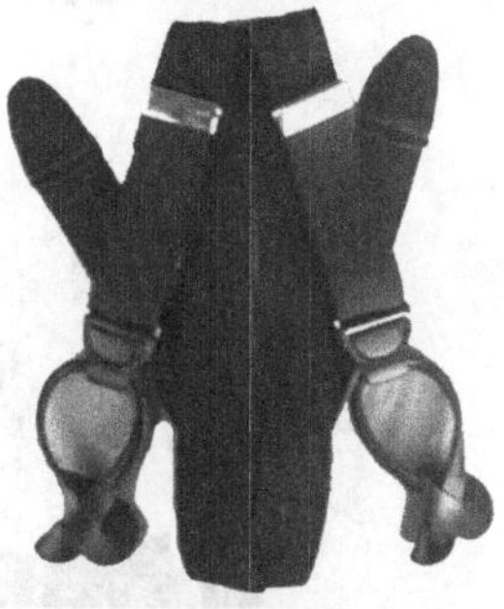

suspenders

If the invitation says "Black Tie Optional", it is not as strict a requirement for formal attire as "Black Tie" or "Black Tie Preferred", yet formal dress is wholly appropriate and welcome. Styles may include Black Tuxedo, White Dinner Jacket or a dark contemporary style Tuxedo (no Tailcoats).

If the invitation says "Black Tie Invited", which appears more frequently than "Black Tie Preferred" or "Black Tie Optional," it is usually sent out for large gatherings of civic or business groups. It indicates that gentlemen are welcome to dress in formal

Evening separates

Evening gowns or Cocktail dresses

White Dinner Jacket

Black Tuxedo

attire if they would like, but it is not necessary. Styles for these affairs are the same as for "Black Tie Optional."

There are some other dress codes besides "White Tie" and "Black Tie."

"Semi-Formal" or "After Five" means that Tuxedos are not required, nor are long dresses. Daytime semi-formal events call for a suit for a man and an appropriate short dress or dressy suit for a woman. An evening wedding (after 6 pm) would still dictate dark suits for men, and cocktail dresses for women.

"Cocktail Attire" means short, elegant dresses for women and dark suits for men.

2. *Casual wear*

Informal is often considered as the same as Casual but it actually calls for the same dress as Semi-Formal—dark suits for him, short dresses for her—especially when associated with a wedding or special event.

"Dressy Casual" calls for dressed-up versions of casual looks. For a man, it could be trousers and a sport coat, for a woman a dressy pants look. For Dressy Casual, Jeans, shorts, T-shirts and other casual looks are not proper.

In daily leisure time without social events, "casual dress" is very popular, it means one may wear anything as he or she likes. In these informal occasions, comfort, convenience, and beauty may be greatly taken into consideration rather than dressing etiquette.

Casual wear

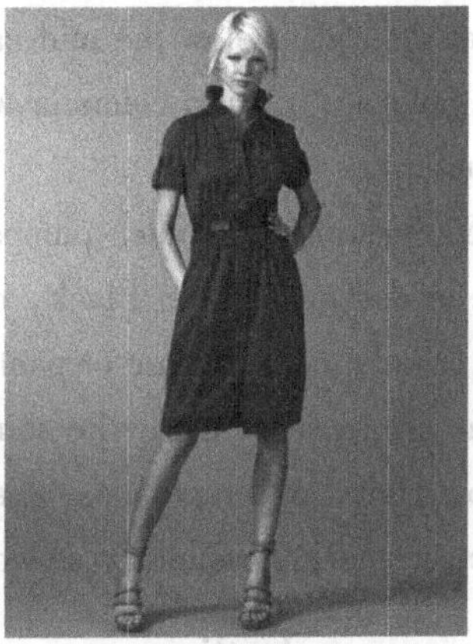

Casual dress

3. *Formal Business Attire*

Formal business attire is often adopted in formal business occasion. The following are some suggested attires for men and women respectively:

Men's Formal business attire:

- Suit: a clean, pressed, solid-colored, conservative suit whose color varies from dark blue to gray or one in subtle pinstripe or plaid
- Shirts—long-sleeved non-flashy shirt in solid colors such as white, cream, or light blue

- Tie—in solids, stripes, and small patterns and the tip of it should reach but not beyond the top of the belt
- Shoes & Socks—slip-on shoes and lace-up shoes in black or dark brown with dark or neutral color over-the-calf socks
- Hair & Skin—hair should be clean and neatly combed and the face should be shaven

***Women's Formal business attire*:**

- Suit: matched-skirted suit in neutral colors such as grey, blue, or black or plaids, or a simple tailored suit or dress. The length of the skirt should be no shorter than slightly above the knee, no longer than just below the mid-calf.
- Blouses: blouses in solid colors or with simple patterns. White, ivory, or light blue are much preferred.
- Shoes & Stockings: Leather pumps. The color of the shoes should match with the hemline or darker than it. Black, navy, dark brown and maroon are much preferred. Neutral or nude colored hose or panty hose which may easily match or compliment one's skin tone always accompany the skirt.
- Makeup, Hair, & Fragrance: wear moderate makeup or perfume. Hair should be clean, neat and professionally styled and in natural color.

4. *Business casual attire*

Business casual, which is also called "smart casual", is usually more relaxed, yet still professional. It originated in white—collar workplaces in western countries in the 1990s. Business casual is a middle ground between business formal wear and street wear. The definition of it differs widely between organizations and places. Some examples are as follows:

***Men's Business casual*:**

- The top: blazers, sport coats, button-down shirts, polo shirts, sweaters

- The bottom: khaki or flannel pants, jeans (if allowed)
- Shoes: leather shoes, sneakers (if allowed)

Button-down shirt

Polo shirt

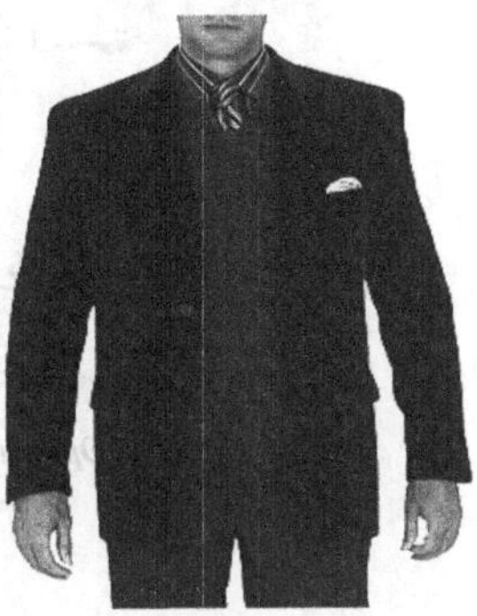

Sport coat

Women's Business casual:

- The top: Blazers, twin sets, turtlenecks, shirts, blouses, sweaters

Twin sets

Turtleneck

- The bottom: pants, simple skirts in solid tones or subtle patterns, jeans (if allowed)
- Shoes: open-toed heels, slingbacks, loafers, open-toed pumps, sneakers (if allowed)

Whether jeans and sneakers are acceptable in business occasion is not so definite, some organizations frown upon them as too casual, some consider them usual.

Some tips of the etiquette of dressing:

- If you are not quite sure about what to wear on some occasion, go towards formality.
- It is a good manner to take off one's coat and hat after entering one's house.

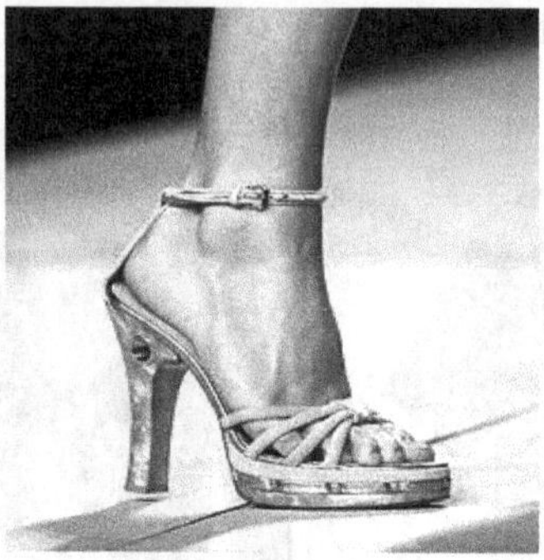

Open-toed heels

Slingbacks

Loafers

Open-toed pumps

- It is polite for the host or hostess to help the guest to take off his or her coat on entering and to put on the coat when leaving.
- If a man is wearing gloves, he should take off the gloves from his right hand before shaking hands, if this is difficult to do so for certain reason, he must say, "Excuse my glove", while a woman need not take off her glove.
- It is not polite for the host or hostess to meet guests in pyjamas and slippers.
- In formal social occasion, a men should manage to dress himself almost the same as other men around, while a woman should have herself dressed uniquely.
- It is not polite to comb one's hair, apply make-up, clip nails or polish nail polish in public.

Words and Expressions

attire	*n.* 服装
pervasive	*adj.* 普遍深入的
deviate	*v.* 偏离
satin	*n.* 缎子

stripe	*n.* 斑纹,条纹
pique	*n.* 一种针织面料
stud	*n.* 钮扣,饰钮
patent leather shoes	黑漆皮鞋
suspender	*n.* 吊裤带
ballerina	*n.* 芭蕾舞服
pumps	后跟中等或很高的无带女鞋,轻便舞鞋
sandal	*n.* 凉鞋,便鞋
bracelet	*n.* 手镯
cloak	*n.* 半蓬,宽大外衣
stole	*n.* 女用披肩
dressy	*adj.* 衣着考究的
full dress	*n.* 礼服
tuxedo	*n.* 男士无尾半正式晚礼服
symphony	*n.* 交响乐
solid-colored	*a.* 纯白的
wing collar	硬翻领,上浆翻领
pleat	*n.* 褶,褶状物　*vt.* 使…打褶
cocktail dress	*n.* (正式场合穿的)短裙
cufflink	*n.* 男子衬衫袖的链扣
civic	*adj.* 市的,市民的
pinstripe	*n.* 细条纹,细条纹的布料
plaid	*n.* 格子花呢披肩,格子花呢
over-the-calf	高于小腿的
hemline	(裙子、衣服等的)底边,贴边
maroon	*n.* 栗色　*adj.* 栗色的

panty hose	裤袜
skin tone	肤色
blazer 夹克	*n.* 颜色鲜明的运动
button down shirt	领下角有领的衬衫
polo shirt	球衣
flannel	*n.* 法兰绒
dinner jacket	无尾礼服
flashy	*adj.* 浮华的
hose	*n.* 长筒袜
lace – up	*adj.* 系带的 *n.* 系带靴(或鞋)
loafer	*n.* 平底便鞋
middle ground	*n.* 妥协,中间立场
morning dress	*n.* (男式)常礼服
navy	*n.* 深蓝色
nude colored	肉色的
nail polish	*n.* 指甲油
slip-on	*adj.* 容易穿或脱的,自头部套上的(衣服,鞋子)
sport coat	*n.* 运动服上装
sneaker	*n.* 运动鞋,旅游鞋
tailocat	*n.* 燕尾服
tailored suit	女士西服
taupe	*n.* 灰褐色 *adj.* 褐色的
twin set	*n.* 女式两件套
turtleneck	*n.* 套领,套领毛衣

Part III Sample Dialogues

Sample Dialogue 1: *At the garment department*

A: Will you try this suit for size, sir?

B: Oh, it seems a little too narrow across the shoulders, a little tight through the back. And the trousers are a bit narrow in the seat.

A: Sorry, this is the XXL size. I'm afraid our ready-made sizes are just a little too small for you.

B: what a pity! I like this style very much.

A: How about ordering a suit tailor-made? Clothes that are made to measure fit the body perfectly, and there is minor difference in the price between a ready-made suit and a tailored one.

B: How much is it if I order a suit?

A: I may give you a 10% discount, we could tailor one for you for about 500 yuan.

B: OK, I will get one made.

Sample Dialogue 2: *What to Wear on a Wedding*?

A: I've got the invitation to one of my friends' wedding, but what am I supposed to wear?

B: The etiquette for proper wedding guest attire can vary greatly depending on the style and time of the wedding.

A: It reads "Black Tie Optional".

B: Is it a daytime wedding or an evening one?

A: An evening one.

B: A black cocktail dress is fine, not too sexy or revealing, you should avoid white color.

A: why?

B: It is often the color of the wedding dress of the bride, since she is the only heroine of the wedding, the guest should not clash with her in the color of the dresses.

A: I see. Then, how about the shoes? It is an outdoor wedding.

B: You'd better avoid high heeled shoes that will sink in the sand or in the grass.

Sample Dialogue 3: *What to Wear at a Job Interview*?

A: I will receive a job interview in a big company next Monday. Can you give me some suggestions about what to wear?

B: Sure. From the moment you meet your interviewer, your appearance and body language are sending cues about the kind of employee you will be. The first impression is very important.

A: I can't agree with you more. I prepared two suits, one is gray and the other is dark blue, which one is better?

B: The latter is better. It shows your staidness(沉着).

A: Yes. Then what kind of tie is proper?

B: You'd better choose one in small pattern, not too bright and the tip of it should reach but not beyond the top of the belt.

A: Is it right for me to wear a pair of black patent leather shoes?

B: Fine, it will match your dark blue well.

A: Thanks.

B: You are welcome! I hope you have a successful interview.

Sample Dialogue 4: *Do I Look Ok*?

A: Hey, that's a really nice outfit you have on.

B: Thank you. I wasn't sure if it looked OK or not.

A: Oh, you look stunning(极好的). Your dress really goes well with your shoes.

B: I'm glad that you think so. I think it might be a bit revealing.

A: No, not at all. You look really elegant in it. Where did you pick that up?

B: At the department store. You should go there to take a look. They have both casual and formal styles.

A: I might just do that. Anyway, are you going to wear that outfit to the party this evening?

B: I don't think so. It is a little too formal. I'm probably going to wear something more casual.

A: Me too. I will probably go dressed in a T-shirt and jeans.

B: I guess that you will really be dressing down.

A: That's my style when I am not in the office.

B: All right. I suppose that we all have our own individual style and the party is not such a formal one.

Part IV Follow-up Practice

1. ***Pair-work: discuss and conclude the proper attire for a professional woman in her work place.***
2. ***Role play: An overweight lady can't find a ready-made cocktail dress in her size for a party. The shop assistant suggests that she order a dress tailored and recommends some styles and colors to her. You may refer to sample dialogue 1.***

Part V Reading for Fun

Benefit of Owning a Company

Employed by the human-development center of a corporation in the Midwest, my friend trains employees in proper dress codes and etiquette.

One day as she was stepping onto the elevator, a man casually dressed in jeans and a golf shirt got on with her.

Thinking of her responsibilities, she scolded, "Dressed a little casually today, aren't we?"

The man replied, "That's one benefit of owning the company..."

Part VI Supplementary Reading

The Story of Blue Jeans

Although denim(粗斜纹棉布) pants had been around as work wear for many years, historically dating back to England in the 1600s with a fabric there called denim, it was the first use of rivets rivet (铆钉) that created what we now call jeans. "Waist overalls" was the traditional name for work pants, which is what these first jeans were called. The word jeans became more popular around 1960 when the baby-boom generation adopted the term for its favorite type of pants.

The following is a story of the invention of blue jeans.

Levi Strauss, who was a twenty-four-year old young man then, came to San Francisco in 1853 to open a west coast branch of his brothers' New York dry goods business. He had spent a number of years learning the trade in New York after emigrating there from his native Germany. He built his business into a very successful operation over the next twenty years, making a name for himself not only as a well-respected businessman, but as a local philanthropist(慈善家) as well.

One of Levi's many customers was a tailor named Jacob Davis who regularly purchased bolts of cloth from the wholesale house of Levi Strauss & Co. Among Jacob's customers there was a man who kept ripping the pockets of the pants that Jacob made for him. Jacob tried to think of a way to strengthen the man's trousers, and one day he hit upon the idea of putting metal rivets at the points of strain, such as on the pocket corners and at the base of the button fly.

These riveted pants were an instant hit with Jacob's customers and he worried that someone might steal this great idea. He thought he should apply for a patent on the process, but he didn't have the $68 that was required to file the papers. He needed a business partner and he immediately thought of Levi Strauss.

In 1872 Jacob wrote a letter to Levi to suggest that they two hold the patent together. Levi, who was an astute(机敏的) businessman, saw the potential for this new product and agreed to Jacob's proposal. On May 20, 1873, the two men received patent from the U. S. Patent and Trademark Office. That day is now considered to be the official "birthday" of blue jeans.

With the patent secured, Levi hired Jacob Davis to oversee production of the riveted pants at the Levi Strauss & Co. San Francisco plant. Sometime during 1873, the first riveted clothing was made and sold. Jacob Davis was in charge of manufacturing when Levi Strauss & Co. opened its two San Francisco factories.

The denim for the riveted work pants came from the Amoskeag Mill in Manchester, New Hampshire, a company known for the quality of its fabrics. Within a very short time, all types of working men were buying the innovative new pants and spreading the word about their unrivaled(无敌的,至高无上的) durability.

Holding a patent (专利) on this process meant that for nearly twenty years, Levi Strauss & Co. was the only company allowed to make riveted clothing until the patent went into the public domain. Around 1890, these pants were assigned the number 501, which they still bear today. When the patent expired dozens of garment manufacturers began to imitate the original riveted clothing made popular by Levi Strauss & Co.

In the 1950s, high school kids put them on as a radical way of defining themselves, of wanting to look and be more adult — and dangerous and rebellious against adults because adults didn't wear jeans. A decade later, blue jeans became a symbol of egalitarianism(平等主义), a uniform for young adult baby boomers waging a generational war. In the 1970s Me Decade and the beginnings of celebrity culture surfaced, jeans were definitely about being sexy and all about fashion. Acceptance of jeans continued through the 1980s and 1990s to the point where jeans are now a wardrobe staple, with the average North American owning seven pairs.

The term "Levi's" though, was not the company's—it originated with the public, just as the public invented the term "coke" for Coca-Cola. But when the public started referring to the pants generically as "Levi's", the company quickly trademarked it. No item of clothing is more American than the blue jeans invented and perfected in the last quarter of the 19th century by Jacob Davis and Levi Strauss These two visionary immigrants, turned denim, thread and a little metal into the most popular clothing product in the world—blue jeans.

Part VII Useful Words and Expressions

breeches 马裤	jerkin 猎装
bathing trunks 游泳裤	knickers 短裤，灯笼裤
swimsuit 游泳衣	maxiskirt （长至脚踝的）超长裙
bikini 比基尼泳衣	miniskirt 迷你短裙，超短裙
bathrobe 浴衣	overcoat 男式大衣
between seasons wear 春秋衫	overalls 工装裤

blouse　女式衬衫	petticoat　衬裙
briefs/ shorts/ panties　短内裤,三角裤	round-neck sweater　圆领运动衫
braces　裤子背带	scarf, muffler　围巾
bra　胸衣	shawl　大披巾
coat　大衣	suit/ outfit/ ensemble　套服
cape coat / dust coat　风衣	slip　套裙
dressing gown　晨衣（美作:duster）	stockings　长袜
cardigan　开襟毛衣	socks　短袜
dress/ one-piece dress　连衣裙	slim skirt/ qipao　旗袍裙
divided skirt, split skirt　裙裤	sleeveless garment　马甲
double-breasted suit　双排扣外衣	tailored suit　女式西服
dinner jacket　无尾礼服（美作:tuxedo）	three-piece suit　三件套
down garment　羽绒服	three-quarter coat　中长大衣
evening dress　夜礼服	topcoat　夹大衣
everyday clothes　便服	underwear, underclothes　内衣裤
formal dress　礼服	underpants, pants　内衣裤（美作:shorts）
fur coat　皮大衣	waistcoat　背心
garments/ town clothes　外衣	wool sweater　羊毛衫
Jacket　夹克	
You really look beautiful/ handsome/ nice/ pretty in the dress/ purple. 您穿这件衣服/紫色衣服看起来很漂亮/帅气。	It is non-crushable.（抗皱的）
Your tie matches your suit well. 这条领带和你的西装很搭配。	It wears well. 耐穿的

Keys for Lead-in Exercises

1. 1) E　2) A　3) B　4) D　5) C

Unit 5

The Etiquette at Wedding Ceremony

Part I Lead-in Exercises

1. ***Have you ever attended or witnessed Western-style wedding? If yes, tell your partner how it looks like and how you feel about it. If not, imagine what it is like according to the knowledge you've got.***

2. ***Vocabulary building: Match the Chinese words on the left column with their appropriate English expressions on the right.***

1) 婚誓	A. wedding ceremony
2) 蜜月	B. bride
3) 伴郎	C. bridegroom or groom
4) 牧师	D. officiator
5) 新娘	E. pastor
6) 结婚典礼	F. groomsman
7) 婚宴	G. bridesmaid
8) 伴娘	H. honeymoon
9) 主婚人	I. wedding reception
10) 新郎	J. vows

1) ________ 2) ________ 3) ________ 4) ________ 5) ________
6) ________ 7) ________ 8) ________ 9) ________ 10) ________

Part II Wedding Etiquette

The wedding day is the bride and groom's special day. If each guest displays courtesy and thoughtfulness, the day will be a smooth and enjoyable experience for everyone in attendance. The following passages will be about some basics of wedding guest etiquette that will help you to ensure that you don't inadvertently commit a faux pas or do anything mistaken at a loved one's wedding.

1. *Responding Promptly*

When you receive your invitation, there will be an "RSVP" date imprinted on the bottom. RSVP is French for repondez s'il vous plait, or quite simply "please respond." The couple will be making many decisions based on the number of people who will be there. Additionally, if you must cancel after you have accepted, do so as soon as possible.

While it's considered very bad manners to respond after RSVP date, it's even worse to show up at the wedding after having not replied at all.

2. *Be Punctual*

Don't be late! If a wedding invitation says that the ceremony will begin at 5, be sure to arrive there by 4:45 so as to give yourself time to find a seat and get settled.

If you are late and the processional or ceremony has already started, take your cue from the wedding coordinator or church coordinator. They will allow you to enter when there is opportunity to do so. If the processional is in progress, don't interrupt. Instead, wait until the wedding party has entered, then quietly slip in a side door and choose a seat in the back. Do not enter down the center aisle unless there is no other option.

3. *Dress Appropriately*

If the ceremony will be held in a church, guests may not be able to wear sundresses, short skirts, shorts, and other revealing or casual attire, including baseball caps. Do not wear caps, jeans, or shorts to any wedding except a very informal outdoor gathering.

A daytime wedding always calls for a short dress unless the function is ultra-formal. You can wear hats and gloves if the wedding is formal. For an informal or semi-formal evening wedding, wear a cocktail dress. For a formal wedding, look for a long cocktail dress. You can wear a gown to an ultra-formal evening wedding.

As a guest, find out what color the bridesmaids will be wearing, and choose something else. You don't want to be competing with the wedding party for attention.

Never, ever wear a long white dress to someone else's wedding! It competes with the bride. Even if the bride will be wearing something other than white, it is still considered in bad taste for a guest to choose this color.

For men, it is much easier to dress themselves for this special occasion. Black tie can be safe all the time.

4. *Sending Gifts*

The purpose of inviting guests is to have them witness a couple's marriage ceremony and vows and to share in the bride and groom's joy and celebration. Gifts for the bride and groom are optional, although most guests attempt to give at least a token gift of their best wishes. While it's no need to bring gifts to the wedding, a wedding present for the Happy Couple is indeed required. Whether it's a monetary gift or something purchased from a registry, you have up to a year from the wedding date to see the bride and groom receive it. Many wedding guests choose to give monetary gifts to the Happy Couple on the day of the wedding; others choose to send gifts ahead of time or very soon after the wedding. Either way is fine as long as you give a gift. If you won't be attending the wedding, it's still customary to send a gift.

5. *Being Polite at the Wedding Ceremony*

- Being Considerate: Don't carry on a conversation with the person next to you while you are seated in church or crack jokes with the person across the pew. Be considerate of the Happy Couple and all others in attendance.
- Taking Pictures: Do not rise up frequently to take pictures during the ceremony. Many churches do not allow flash pictures and you may disturb the ceremony. The professional photographer is the only one who should be taking pictures and he/she will know the rules of the church or event center.
- Getting to know when to stand or sit: At most ceremonies, the guests stand when the bride enters. Remain standing until the officiant asks you to be seated. When the ceremony ends, remain in your seat until the ushers dismiss you, or if there are no ushers, until the mothers of the bride and groom have been escorted out. Allow family members of the bride and groom, who will be seated near the front, to exit first.
- Do remember to turn your cell phone on silent and let calls go to voice mail. Your phone's ring tone will certainly land you in the wedding guest hall of shame.

6. *Behaving Yourself Properly*

- It's considered poor wedding guest etiquette to call the bride or groom to ask if you can bring a guest. Don't bring anyone who is not included in the invitation letter.
- Do introduce yourself to everyone at your table at the reception, and make polite conversation, i. e. you might ask how he or she knows the bride or groom.
- Don't pile your plate full unless you are at the end of the line, if a buffet is served at the reception. Be courteous of those who have yet to eat.
- Don't drink too much. You are there to celebrate with the newlyweds, not embarrass yourself and them.

7. *More Worth Mentioning*

- Inviting a date to escort: If, when you receive your invitation, the words "and guest" appear written next to your name on the envelope, you can feel free to invite a date to escort you to the wedding. If the words "and guest" don't appear on your envelope, expect to attend this event alone. Because the Happy Couple has to pay by the head,

they might not be able to afford to invite extra people. The only time it is assumed a significant other is invited is if one is married, engaged, or living with another party.

- Bringing Children: If you bring children, keep them under control. During the reception, don't allow the children to run wild. Don't expect the photographer, coordinator, or DJ to supervise them for you. If your children cause damage, be prepared to pay for it. Otherwise, the bride and groom will be held responsible and friendships could be ruined.

Words and Expressions

courtesy	*n.* 谦恭，允许，礼貌
processional	*adj.* 游行的 *n.* 游行圣歌，仪式
inadvertently	*adv.* 不注意地
monetary	*adj.* 货币的，金钱的
officiant	*n.* 主祭
escort	*n.* 护卫（队），护送，陪同（人员）
faux pas	*n.* 失言，失礼，失态

Part III Sample Dialogues

Sample Dialogue 1: Before the Wedding

Shrilly: Have you heard about Diana?

Vince: No, I haven't talked to her for a couple of months. How are things with her?

Shrilly: Well, she is just so-so right now. She had a little accident last week in her new car.

Vince: Oh, you are kidding. Was anybody hurt? Was there much damage?

Shrilly: No, it was really a small accident and everybody was fine. It was the other driver's fault.

Vince: Well, that's good. Other than that, how's she doing? Is she still going out with Steve?

Shrilly: Haven't you heard yet? They're getting married!

Vince: You are kidding!

Shrilly: She said he gave her a ring on her birthday.

Vince: That's great!

Shrilly: Yeah. Everybody's really happy about it. He is a great guy.

Vince: Lucky, too.

Sample Dialogue 2: On Wedding Day

Diana: I would prefer a sincere affair of a few people. Here you really felt that it was a meaningful thing, and not just a showy(炫耀的,卖弄的) prestigious(享有声望的) affair for... for parents to show off what they can provide for their daughters or son.

Tom: But that's an important thing for the parents to do, isn't it? I mean, parents at that ... it ought to be ... parents ought to be allowed to do this.

Diana: But one is getting married, not one's parents.

Tom: Yes, but it's the parents who are paying for it. And it's the parents who've, if you like,... brought up this young girl or man to ...

Diana: Surely the money that is spent ... I'd prefer to see the money spent on something more worthwhile.

Tom: Yes, but it's not ... it may not be your money as such. And I think if the parents are paying for it, then they should have a great deal to say about it. If they prefer a large wedding and they prefer to ... to invite Aunty Fole, Uncle Bill who you haven't seen since you were two years old, well, I think that's their prerogative (特权).

Diana: So it really boils down to(归结为) what they prefer rather than what ... the son or daughter prefers ...

Tom: Well, not entirely. But nevertheless I think it is important that they should ... that they be consulted.

Sample Dialogue 3: On Wedding Ceremony

Mary: Hi, Lucy!

Lucy: Hi. It's a wonderful wedding, isn't it?

Mary: Yes, it's great.

Lucy: Julia's father is a rich man, isn't he?

Mary: You are tight, Mary's father is responsible for the entire wedding arrangement, costs, etc. I think he must spend much money.

Lucy: Will Julia and her husband be ready to leave for their honeymoon?

Mary: Yes, they have planned for a long time. They are going to Austria for their honeymoon.

Lucy: So great. Look! Julia is going to throw the bride bouquet(花束).

Mary: Oh, I'll try to catch it. It will bring me good luck.

Sample dialogue 4: Some Marriage Traditions

Lisa: I have surprising news for you.

Billy: What's that?

Lisa: Barbara is getting married.

Billy: Well, isn't that simply wonderful! My best wishes to her. Who's the lucky guy?

Lisa: Jason. He proposed last Saturday night at the formal dance.

Billy: My, how romantic! When is the big day?

Lisa: This August.

Billy: Will it be a church wedding or a civil wedding?

Lisa: Well, Barbara is a catholic. So, there will be a church wedding.

Billy: Good. So Barbara will be a bride. She will be very beautiful in her wedding gown.

Lisa: She's hoping I'll be her maid of honour.

Billy: Did you promise her?

Lisa: Yes, I did. It'll be my first time.

Billy: Who did Jason ask to be his best man?

Lisa: My boyfriend, Tom.

Billy: That's very interesting. The groom's best man is the maid of honour's boyfriend.

Lisa: And they will go to a large restaurant for the reception after the wedding ceremony.

Billy: That will be very expensive for the father of the bridegroom, won't it?

Lisa: No, the bride's family is responsible for the entire wedding arrangements, costs, etc.

Billy: That's why many American fathers joke they would rather hold the ladder for their daughter to climb down and elope(私奔) than pay for a wedding.

Part IV Follow-up Practice

1. ***Guess how many years these items stand for according to what you know.***

Paper wedding	Tin wedding	Crystal wedding	China wedding
Silver wedding	Pearl wedding	Ruby wedding	Sapphire wedding
Golden wedding	Emerald wedding	Diamond wedding	

2. ***Group work: Compare Chinese wedding ceremony with western wedding ceremony. Make a list of their differences.***

3. ***Role play: Let's have a wedding ceremony. Please hold a wedding ceremony after consulting some information about the wedding processional and make it a performance in the class.***

Part V Reading for Fun

Jennifer's wedding day was fast approaching. Nothing could dampen her excitement—not even her parent's nasty divorce. Her mother had found the PERFECT dress to wear and would be the best-dressed mother-of-the-bride ever!

A week later, Jennifer was horrified to learn that her father's new young wife had bought the exact same dress! Jennifer asked her to exchange it, but she refused. "Absolutely not, I look like a million bucks in this dress, and I'm wearing it," she replied.

Jennifer told her mother who graciously said, "Never mind sweetheart. I'll get another dress. After all, it's your special day."

A few days later, they went shopping and did find another gorgeous dress. When they stopped for lunch, Jennifer asked her mother, "Aren't you going to return the other dress? You really don't have another occasion where you could wear it."

Her mother just smiled and replied, "Of course I do, dear. I'm wearing it to the rehearsal dinner the night before the wedding."

Part VI Supplementary Reading

Wedding Processional

The order of wedding processionals follows a general pattern, but varies according to religious traditions. The following is an example of a typical processional order.

- ***The Mothers & Grandmothers***

Just before the ceremony is scheduled to start and the guests have arrived and been seated, the mothers and grandmothers should be seated in the following manner.

First the grandmothers of the groom are seated — escorted by an usher(引座员) and followed by their husbands. Then an usher escorts the grandmothers of the bride. The ushers for the grandmothers should be a member of their family if possible — sons, grandsons, etc.

Next the mother of the groom is ushered to her seat and is followed by her husband, if he is not in the wedding party.

Finally the mother of the bride is seated. The mothers should be escorted by one of their sons or another family member who is an usher or by the best man. The seating of the bride's mother signals that the ceremony is starting. At this point the ushers may roll out an aisle runner if one is being used.

• ***The Officiant & Groom***

After the bride's mother is seated and the wedding procession is formed in the vestibule(门厅), the officiant and the groom enter. They should walk in from the side and stand at the front, facing the guests. If the best man will not be escorting the maid of honor down the aisle, then he should enter with the groom. Traditionally the groom stands on the right side of the aisle with his best man slightly behind him and to his left.

• ***The Attendants***

There are many possibilities as to how the attendants can make their way to the front of the church.

◇The ushers can escort the bridesmaids down the aisle.

◇If the ushers are walking separate from the bridesmaids or if you have more ushers than bridesmaids …

◇The ushers could walk down the aisle first in pairs or alone. Alternatively, the ushers could walk single file down a side aisle and stand at the front of the church facing the guests.

◇The bridesmaids follow either walking in pairs or alone.

◇Finally the maid or matron of honor. If there are both, the matron(主要伴娘) of honor goes first and then the maid of honor — so that the maid of honor stands closest to the bride.

◇Consider having the shortest attendants walk down the aisle first — at the front of the church they should line up with the men on the right and the women on the left and tallest to shortest with the shortest being farthest from the bride and groom.

Note: The hesitation step is a trend of the past. The

attendants should simply walk down the aisle slowly and steadily!

• ***The Flower Girl & Ring Bearer***

If there are one flower girl and one ring bearer, they could always walk together. Another nice alternative is to have two flower girls and one ring bearer; let the girls walk side by side followed by the ring bearer.

The flower girl typically takes her place on the left side of the church next to the maid of honor. The ring bearer typically takes his place on the right side of the church next to the best man. Other arrangements may be made for the children to sit with their parents during the ceremony depending on the child's age and level of maturity.

• ***The Bride***

Finally the time has come... cue(暗示) the music—"Here Comes the Bride"! At this point everyone present should stand and turn to watch the bride and her father their walk down the aisle.

In Christian ceremonies the bride should walk on her father's left. When she reaches the groom's side, her father lets go of her arm and gives her hand to the groom. The congregation remains standing until the father sits down.

Discovering Wedding Customs and Traditions of the Past

The wedding is one of life's primeval(古老的) and surprisingly unchanged rites of passage. Nearly all of the customs in western countries are merely echoes of the past. Everything from the veil, rice, flowers, and old shoes, to the bridesmaids and processionals, at one time, bore a very specific and vitally significant meaning. Today, although the original substance is often lost, the old world customs are incorporated into the weddings because they are traditional and ritualistic(仪式的).

Old world marriage customs continue to thrive today, in diluted(冲淡的), disguised and often upgraded forms. Customs we memorialize today, were once "brand new" ideas. Although historical accuracy is hard to achieve, the historical weight attached to old world wedding customs and traditions is immense.

• ***Why Does the Bride Wear a Veil?***

The bride's veil and bouquet are of greater antiquity(古代的遗物) than her white gown. Her veil, which was yellow in ancient Greece and red in ancient Rome, usually shrouded(遮蔽) her from head to foot, and has since the earliest of times, denoted(指示,表示) the subordination of a woman to man. The thicker the veil, the more traditional the implication of wearing it.

According to tradition, it is considered bad luck for the bride to be seen by the groom before the ceremony. As a matter of fact, in the old days of marriage by purchase, the couple rarely saw each other at all, with courtship being of more recent historical emergence.

The lifting of the veil at the end of the ceremony symbolizes male dominance. If the bride takes the initiative in lifting it, thereby presenting herself to him, she is showing more independence.

Veils came into vogue(时尚,流行) in the United States when Nelly Curtis wore a veil at her wedding to George Washington's aid, Major Lawrence Lewis. Major Lewis saw his bride to be standing behind a filmy curtain and commented to her how beautiful she appeared. She then decided to veil herself for their ceremony.

• ***Why the Honeymoon?***

In ancient times, many of the first marriages were by capture, not choice. When early man felt it was time to take a bride, he would often carry off an unwilling woman to a secret place where her relatives wouldn't find them. While the moon went through all its phases, (about 30 days) they hid from the searchers and drank a brew made from honey. Hence, we get the word, honeymoon.

• ***Why Does the Bride Wear White?***

The color white has been a symbol of joyous celebration since early Roman times. At the beginning to the twentieth century, white stood for purity as well. Today, it holds it original meaning of happiness and joy.

• ***Why Does the Bride Carry Flowers?***

For centuries, flowers have stood for a variety of emotions and values. Roses for love, lilies for virtue and so on. In ancient marriages, the brides carried herbs beneath their veils to symbolize fidelity(忠实，忠诚). Greek brides carried ivy as a symbol of never-ending love. Orange blossoms, (the world renowned wedding flower) were chosen by the Spaniards to represent happiness and fulfillment, because the orange tree flowers and bears fruit at the same time. During even earlier times of "primitive marriage," when the fear of demons was most prevalent, the brides carried stinking garlands of herbs and spices for the purpose of frightening off evil spirits.

Today, brides carry flowers in the color scheme of their wedding, bringing beauty and elegance as well as old world customs to their special day.

• ***Why the Third Finger, Left-hand?***

In ancient times, it was believed there was a vein in the third finger of the left hand that ran directly to the heart. Thus, the ring being placed on that finger denoted the strong connection of a heartfelt love and commitment to one another. Although during times of modern autopsy(人体解剖), this long held belief was found not to be so, the tradition continued to this day.

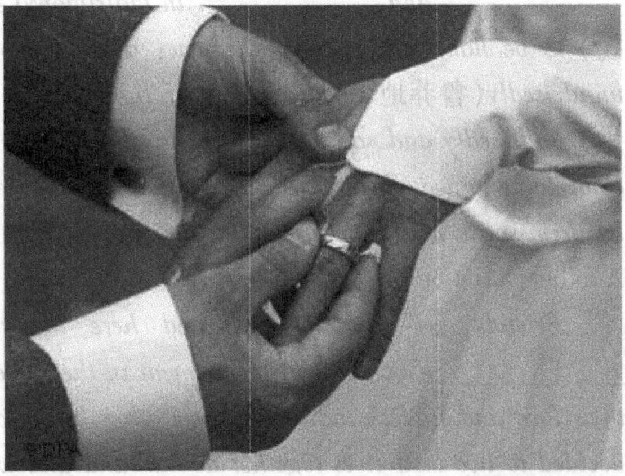

Medieval bridegrooms place the ring on three of the bride's fingers, in turn, to symbolize, God the Father, God the Son and God the Holy Spirit. The ring then remained on the third finger and has become the customary ring finger for English-speaking cultures. In some European countries, the ring is worn on the left hand before marriage, and is moved to the right hand during the ceremony. However, in most European countries the ring is still worn on the bride's left hand. A Greek Orthodox bride wears her ring on her left hand before marriage, and moves it to her right hand after the ceremony.

• ***Why a Wedding Ring?***

The circular shape of the wedding ring has symbolized undying, unending love since the days of the early Egyptians. A primitive bride wore a ring of hemp(纤维) or rushes (灯芯草), which had to be replaced often. Durable iron was used by the Romans to symbolize the permanence of marriage. Today's favorite is of course, gold, with it's lasting qualities of beauty and purity.

Part VII Useful Words and Expressions

Wedding Vows and Other Expressions

Opening words of the officiant

The wedding should begin by welcoming the guests. In movies, we often hear:

Dearly Beloved, we are gathered here today in the presence of these witnesses, to join __________ and __________ in matrimony(结婚), which is commended(称赞，表扬) to be honorable among all men; and therefore—is not by any—to be entered into unadvisedly(鲁莽地，欠思虑的) or lightly—but reverently(虔诚地), discreetly(谨慎地), advisedly and solemnly. Into this holy estate(时期) these two persons present now come to be joined. If any person can show just cause why they may not be joined together—let them speak now or forever hold their peace.

Another variation is:

Friends, we have been invited here today to share with __________ and __________ a very important moment in their lives. In the years they have been together, their love and understanding of each other has grown and matured, and now they have decided to live their lives together as husband and wife.

Wedding vows

• "Will you, __________, have ________ to be your wife/husband? Will you love her/him, comfort and keep her/him, and forsaking(放弃，抛弃)all other remain true to him/her as long as you both shall live?" ("I will")

- (Repeat) "I, ____________, take thee ____________, to be my wife/husband, and before God and these witnesses I promise to be a faithful and true wife/husband."
- (Rings) "With this ring I thee wed(结婚), and all my worldly goods I thee endow(赋予). In sickness and in health, in poverty or in wealth, 'til death do us part."

Keys for Lead-in Exercises

2.1)J 2)H 3)F 4)E 5)B 6)A 7)I 8)G 9)D 10)C

Follow-up Practice 1

Paper wedding 纸婚、布婚(结婚一周年)
Tin wedding 锡婚(结婚十周年)
Crystal wedding 水晶婚(结婚十五周年)
china wedding 搪瓷婚(结婚二十周年)
Silver wedding 银婚(结婚二十五周年)第一大典
Pearl wedding 珍珠婚(结婚三十周年)
Ruby wedding 红宝石婚(结婚四十周年)
Sapphire wedding 蓝宝石婚(结婚四十五周年)
Golden wedding 金婚(结婚五十周年)第二大典
Emerald wedding 翠玉婚(结婚五十五周年)
Diamond wedding 钻石婚(结婚六十～七十五周年)

Unit 6

The Etiquette in Funeral Ceremony

Part I Lead-in Exercises

1. ***Have you known how the western-style funeral is alike? If yes, please share what you know about with your partner. If no, please guess how it looks like.***

2. ***Vocabulary building: Match the Chinese words on the left column with their appropriate English expressions on the right.***

1)国葬	A. state funeral
2)献花圈仪式	B. wreath laying (placing) ceremony
3)向遗体告别	C. to pay final respects
4)(宗)追思礼拜	D. memorial service
5)墓地	E. final rest place
6)挽歌,哀乐	F. dirge
7)吊唁,慰问	G. condolence
8)棺材	H. coffin
9)公墓	I. cemetery
10)逝者, 亡人	J. departed saint

1)__________ 2)__________ 3)__________ 4)__________ 5)__________

6)__________ 7)__________ 8)__________ 9)__________ 10)__________

Part II Funeral Etiquette

Funerals serve several purposes. In addition to commemorating the life of the deceased, a funeral offers emotional support to the bereaved and an opportunity for friends and family to pay tribute to their loved one. The process of going through the planning and final disposition helps the family come to terms with the fact that a death has occurred. This is a necessary part of the grieving process. Friends offering fond remembrances, are often helpful during this time. There's certain etiquette to be followed when someone passes away. It's best to know what to expect to avoid acting in an inappropriate manner.

1. *Paying a Visit*

Upon learning of a passing, it's proper to pay your respects to the grieving family in the form of a visit, offering sympathy and asking if you can help. Depending on the family's religion or heritage, this can either be done at home or at the funeral home. Generally, people may prefer to visit the family at the funeral home. This setting may be more comfortable for guests and the family, as they are prepared for visitors. Letting the family know you are there for them and offering your assistance can be a source of comfort to the bereaved, conveying information that while their loved one is gone, they are not alone; that while suffering a great loss, they are still connected to the living, and that life will go on. The visit doesn't have to last long, perhaps fifteen to thirty minutes or so, just enough to express sympathy and let the family know you care. When attending calling hours, do not feel you have to stay for a lengthy period of time. Follow your instincts as to how long to stay. If the deceased was a good friend, you may feel it necessary to stay longer, to tend to your own grief at the same time as paying your respects to the family.

2. *Expressing Sympathy*

Simple, brief expressions of sympathy are usually best. While most people find themselves at a loss for words, the family will appreciate a sincere expression of condolence-however brief. "I'm sorry" or, "I'm so sorry to hear of your loss" are the most commonly used expressions, and they are perfectly adequate when said in a sincere, sympathetic voice. If you knew the deceased well enough, it is often helpful to say so: "I always regarded Jane as a good friend" or, "Tom will be missed by everyone." Kind words are always welcomed. Follow the lead of the family member. If they want to talk about the deceased, lend an ear and a few minutes of your time. Being a good listener may be the best solace you can provide for them.

If you have never met the family, introduce yourself and let them know how you are connected to their loved one. Colleagues and co-workers of the deceased may attend calling hours together, but try not to descend on the bereaved all together. Offer individual sympathy and a word or two of support: "I am so sorry for your loss," and/or, "Let me know if there is anything I can do to help."

Many times funerals become a place to share memories. Visitors are encouraged to talk about their memories of the deceased. Sometimes the family learns new things about their loved one that they didn't know before! While we all accept the somber atmosphere of a funeral setting, sharing stories and laughter can personalize the occasion and actually help ease the pain. Sorrow is an individual suffering, but joyful stories shared freely can make the grief easier to bear.

3. *Offering Help*

If, indeed, you are able to offer assistance with childcare, or food gifts, or picking up out-of-town relatives, by all means, do so. These thoughtful gestures are invaluable. Sudden, or tragic deaths, may be so emotionally draining, your ability to assist the bereaved will be long remembered and appreciated. In the case of the elderly woman or man who has lost a spouse and may not have children close by to attend to their needs, a lending hand with transportation or running errands, can make the ordeal so much easier on them.

4. *Dressing Properly*

A funeral ceremony is definitely a somber affair often requiring a strict funeral dress code. However, having a dress code does not mean that it should be bereft of all style. The basic rule remains that the dress should be black. Nevertheless, you can add a few variations depending upon the prevalent style and the relationship with the deceased.

Women should always stick to the traditional style if they want to feel "safe" within the norms. The best is a black suit where both trousers and skirt can be used. In case it is possible, the best choice for a summer funeral dress for women would be to wear a plain black cocktail dress.

For winter funeral dress attire, it would be good to wear black sweater with black skirt or trousers and closed back shoes. Be particular about not wearing open-toe shoes at a funeral ceremony. The hat, if at all you want to wear one, would be one with a very wide brim and always black.

Men too will have to follow the basic funeral dress code. It is expected of men who are close relatives to wear black suit and white shirt with a plain black tie. For other close friends, it could be all black attire—black turtle neck sweater and black suit or black shirt, black tie and black suit.

Men are advised not to wear any other color suit than black. For footwear, men should wear black socks and black shoes plain and somber looking shoes. Avoid sneakers at all costs. These will look loud and disrespectful among the sea of black dresses usually found at the funerals.

It is becoming more acceptable to wear brighter colors today, to celebrate the life of the deceased , but remember: Do not wear too bright color clothing, such as red, pink, electric blue or the like. Do not wear T-shirts without checking out with the family whether it is okay or not.

5. *Viewing the Body*

In funeral services, a viewing (sometimes called reviewal, funeral visitation or a wake in the United States and Canada) is the time that the family and friends come to see the deceased after they have been prepared by a funeral home. A viewing may take place at the funeral parlour, in a family home or at a church or chapel prior to the actual funeral service.

Viewing is sometimes combined with a celebration of the deceased's life called a wake although in some places the term wake is interchangeable with viewing. Many authorities consider the viewing important to the grieving process as it gives a chance to say goodbye on a personal level. It also can make it easier for the family and the friends to accept the reality of the death. But for the friends, viewing is not required. If you wish to have a family member escort you to the casket, don't be afraid to ask. Regardless of your religious affiliation, a few moments of silence is always appreciated.

6. *Mourning at the Funeral*

A memorial service, often called a funeral and often officiated by clergy from the decedent's or bereaved's church or religion. A funeral may take place at either a funeral home or church. A funeral is held according to the family's choosing which may be a few days after the time of death, allowing family members to attend the service.

Usually a few people who are special to the deceased are chosen to be pallbearers. It's an honor to be chosen and gives the pallbearer one more occasion to do something special for the dearly departed. A member of the clergy will probably conduct the ceremony, but it isn't at all uncommon for friends and family to say a few words about the deceased or read poems or even sing a song, which details happy memories and accomplishments; often commenting on the deceased's flaws, especially at length, is considered impolite. Sometimes the delivering of the eulogy is done by the clergy. Church bells may also be tolled both before and after the service.

Tradition also allows the attendees of the memorial service to have one last opportunity to view the decedent's body and say good-bye; the immediate family, followed by the decedent's spouse, parents and children, are always the very last to view their loved one before the coffin is closed. This opportunity can take place immediately before the service begins, or at the very end of the service.

Funeral customs vary from country to country. In some religious denominations, for example, Roman Catholic and Anglican, eulogies are prohibited or discouraged during this service, in order to preserve respect for traditions. Also, for these religions, the coffin is traditionally closed at the end of the wake and is not re-opened for the funeral service.

7. *Other Means to Express Sympathy*

Besides visiting, there are many other ways to express the sympathy.

- E-mail: E-mail is appropriate from those who are not intimate with the family such as a business associate or a former neighbor. The family will appreciate the message of concern.
- Phone Calls: If you live out-of-town you should telephone as soon as possible to offer your sympathy. Keep the call brief, since others will probably be trying to call as well.
- Flowers: Flowers can be a great comfort to the family and may be sent to the funeral home or to the residence. When ordering flowers, it is important to have an appropriate selection—certain flowers (particularly chrysanthemums or white lilies) are given specially at funerals. To reflect the interests of the family, personalized and creative arrangements will add to the uniqueness of the individual's service.
- Food for the Family: The most welcome gift at this time is food. Also, there may be several visitors in the house who need to be fed. During the days immediately following the death, substantial dishes that require little preparation other than reheating are appropriate.
- Memorial Gifts: A memorial gift is always appropriate, especially when the family has requested such a gift in lieu of flowers.

Usually the family will designate a specific organization or charity. Remember to provide the family's name and address to the charity so they can send proper notification.

- Sympathy Card: Sending a card of sympathy, even if the deceased is only an acquaintance, is good practice and is meaningful to the family.

Words and Expressions

deceased	*adj.* 已故的 *n.* 死者
bereaved	*adj.* 丧失的
tribute	*n.* 颂词
disposition	*n.* 处理
remembrance	*n.* 回想，记忆
condolence	*n.* 哀悼，吊唁
solace	*n.* 安慰
somber	*adj.* 忧郁的
run (on) errands	跑腿，出去办事
ordeal	*n.* 严酷的考验，痛苦的经验，折磨
bereft	*adj.* 被剥夺的，失去亲人的，丧失的
prevalent	*adj.* 普遍的，流行的
brim	*n.* (杯，碗等)边，边缘
sneaker	*n.* 运动鞋
funeral parlour	瞻仰室
interchangeable	*adj.* 可互换的
affiliation	*n.* 联系，从属关系
casket	*n.* (美)棺材
officiate	*v.* 行使

pall bearer	*n.* 护柩者
clergy	*n.* （集合称）圣职者，牧师，神职人员
eulogy	*n.* 赞词，颂词，歌功颂德的话
toll	*vi.* 鸣钟
intimate	*adj.* 亲密的，隐私的
chrysanthemum	*n.* 菊花
substantial	*adj.* 坚固的，实质的，真实的，充实的
in lieu of	代替
designate	*vt.* 指明，任命，指派

Part III Sample Dialogues

Sample Dialogue 1：*At the Hospital*

Sarah： Hello, I was wondering if Tom Smith has checked out yet?

Recept： Just one moment. I'll check with the cancer ward（癌症病房）desk.

Sarah： The cancer ward! Oh, my God. （to Mike） It's worse than we thought.

Recept： Ma'am, I'm sorry. The cancer ward said Mr. Smith passed away two days ago.

Sarah： That's impossible! I'm talking about Mister Tom Smith.

Recept： Yes, Ma'am. He died from complications of stomach cancer. I'm very sorry.

Sarah： （drops the phone） I'm going to be sick!

Mike： Sarah, what's wrong? What happened?

Sarah： Tom's dead. He… had… stomach cancer. It all makes sense now.

Mike： He had stomachaches, headaches, bad moods — and he threw up at the reunion!

Sarah： He had no energy and was so pale and skinny.

Mike： Maybe the hospital got the wrong person! Call Fanny! She works in that cancer ward.

Sarah: OK, I'll call her place. I do hope it is a mistake.

Sample Dialogue 2: *Tom Passed Away*!

Mike: I don't know what to say. This can't be happening. Here's the obituary(讣告).

Sarah: It's really there? It's all one big nightmare.

Mike: But it explains why Tom isn't answering and Fanny took time off from work.

Sarah: Poor Fanny. Tom's death must have made her realize that she still cared for him.

Mike: This says the viewing is at Myers Funeral Home today until five.

Sarah: It's already half past four. We should go and pay our respects. Tom's family will be there.

Mike: Don't we need to give a white envelope with money for the family, though?

Sarah: No. People give plates of food. The food is brought to the reception or in the weeks following.

Mike: At the reception?

Sarah: That's after the funeral. That way the family doesn't need to think about cooking while they're mourning.

Mike: What else can be brought besides food?

Sarah: You can bring flowers if you want.

Sample Dialogue 3: *Say Good-bye to Tom*

FD: I'm sorry, Ma'am. Mr. Smith's viewing is over. It ended an hour ago.

Sarah: But we just drove across town. Can't we just go in to see him one last…

FD: I'm afraid not. But at tomorrow's funeral, the family requested.

Sarah: This is all too fast. He's my best friend, and now he's gone.

FD: I'm sorry. I know it must have come as a great shock.

Sarah: The viewing was for saying goodbye, and I didn't even get that.

FD: It may comfort you to know that many people attended his viewing.

Sarah: How did they hear? No one called.

FD: In times of loss, it is often hard to pick up the phone. But his whole family was here.

Sarah: His mom and dad must be destroyed. He was their only son.

FD: And he was so young, with so much life to look forward to.

Sarah: Yes... thank you for understanding. We have to go now.

FD: This sheet tells the visiting hours and funeral time and location.

Sample Dialogue 4: At the Viewing

Sarah: Oh, no. It looks like we're late.

Mike: Let's just sit in the back. We can still hear the service from here.

Sarah: There're so many people here. Where are Rich and Cath and Tom's parents?

Mike: They're probably up front. The preacher's about to speak. Let's listen.

Sarah: (after the preacher's eulogy) That was such a touching speech. He must have really known Tom well.

Mike: Oh, how I wish this all wasn't happening!

(A man rushes in.)

Tom: Sorry! Excuse me!

Sarah: (surprised) Tom? Tom! Is this a joke? Is it really you? But... but... everyone said you were dead!

Tom: I'm OK! I was out of town with... Fanny.

Sarah: Oh, Tom! I'm so... so happy. But then... (points to the front) who's that?

Tom: Tom Smith. But not me. The pallbearers are carrying out the casket. It would be rude to just leave. Let's follow.

Sarah: It seems so strange to be here, burying you, but it's not you.

Tom: Uh... I'll tell you all about it another day.

Sarah: But you're OK? It was nothing serious, was it?

Tom: You look very elegant in black. But I don't want you to wear black in my honor for a long time yet to come...

Part IV Follow-up Practice

1. ***Look at the following sentences, some of which are often said by people who attend the funeral and some by family members of the departed. Put them into the***

appropriate columns.

Person who attends the funeral	Family members of the departed

1) I'm sorry.
2) Thanks for coming.
3) My sympathy to you.
4) It was good to know John.
5) John talked about you often.
6) John was a fine person and a friend of mine. He will be missed.
7) I didn't realize so many people cared.
8) Come see me when you can.
9) My sympathy to your mother.

2. ***Role play: Your friend Tom has passed away and you're going to attend his funeral. In the funeral, you meet Tom's family members and some friends of both you and Tom. Say something appropriately.***

3. ***Discuss with your partners about Chinese funeral etiquettes. Compare them with those of western cultures and make a list of the differences.***

Part V Reading for Fun

A famous heart specialist doctor died and everyone was gathered at his funeral. A regular coffin was displayed in front of a huge heart.

When the minister finished with the sermon (布道) and after everyone said their good-byes, the heart was opened, the coffin rolled inside, and the heart closed.

Just at that moment one of the mourners started laughing.

The guy next to him asked: "Why are you laughing?"

"I was thinking about my own funeral" the man replied.

"What's so funny about that?"

"I'm a gynecologist(妇科医生)."

Part VI Supplementary Reading

Funeral services differ depending upon the religious and personal beliefs of the family. Funeral services can be held at a church, temple, funeral home, or even the residence. Most folks will choose the funeral home, because of its centralized location.

Whether the service is held at the funeral home or at church, enter quietly and be seated. The first few rows are usually reserved for family members, however, people should sit close behind them to give comfort and support. The ceremony is usually conducted by a member of the clergy, but others may offer thoughts, anecdotes(轶事) or eulogies. The following are about some customs and etiquettes in funeral services.

- ***Music/Violinist***: Music at the service is appropriate. Favorite hymns(赞美诗) or other selections of the deceased can offer comfort to the family. An organist or professionally recorded music is available for a funeral home service. Any musical request for visitation and/or the service should be discussed with the funeral director at the time of arrangements.
- ***Eulogy***: The eulogy adds a personal aspect to the service. It needs not be lengthy, but should offer praise and commendation to the person who has died. It is given by the clergy, a member of the family, a close personal friend or a business associate of the deceased.
- ***Attendance***: Friends and relatives are urged to attend the funeral. The family should consult with the funeral director for an appropriate arrival time. Friends should be considerate of the specified service time and plan to arrive ten to fifteen minutes in advance. Attending the funeral is a simple, but meaningful way to communicate to the family and friends that relatives share their loss.

- ***Funeral Procession***: When the funeral and burial are both held within the local area, it is appropriate for friends and relatives to accompany the family to the cemetery. The procession is formed at the funeral home or church with the car list assignments supervised by the funeral director. Usually the funeral director advises the drivers of procedures to follow when driving in a funeral procession.
- ***Committal***(安放): The family and other persons usually accompany the body to the grave or other place of committal. The clergy or person in charge of the committal offers a short prayer or words of strength prior to committing the body to its final resting place.
- ***Acknowledgements***: The family should promptly acknowledge all flowers and contributions. When food and personal services are provided, these thoughtful acts should also be acknowledged, as should the services of the pallbearers. The funeral director has printed acknowledgement cards, which can be used by the family. When the sender is well known to the family, a short personal note can be written on the acknowledgement card. The note can be short such as: "Thank you for the beautiful roses. The arrangement was most impressive." "The food you sent was so enjoyed by our family. Your kindness is deeply appreciated." "The contribution you sent to the church was a fitting tribute to my husband."

Charles Spencer's Funeral Speech for Diana

The Funeral of Diana, Princess of Wales occurred at Westminster Abbey on Saturday the 6th of September 1997 at 11.00 a.m. Her brother Charles Edward Maurice Spencer, the 9th Earl Spencer delivered the following Tribute for his sister Diana:

I stand before you today the representative of a family in grief, in a country in mourning before a world in shock.

We are all united not only in our desire to pay our respects to Diana but rather in our need to do so. For such was her extraordinary appeal that the tens of millions of people taking part in this service all over the world via television and radio who never actually met her, feel that they too lost someone close to them in the early hours of Sunday morning. It is a more remarkable tribute to Diana than I can ever hope to offer her today.

Diana was the very essence of compassion, of duty, of style, of beauty.

All over the world she was a symbol of selfless humanity. All over the world, a standard-bearer for the rights of the truly downtrodden(被践踏的，被蹂躏的), *a very*

British girl who transcended(超越) nationality. Someone with a natural nobility who was classless and who proved in the last year that she needed no royal title to continue to generate her particular brand of magic.

Today is our chance to say thank you for the way you brightened our lives, even though God granted you but half a life. We will all feel cheated always that you were taken from us so young and yet we must learn to be grateful that you came along at all. Only now that you are gone do we truly appreciate what we are now without, and we want you to know that life without you is very, very difficult. We have all despaired at your loss over the past week and only the strength of the message you gave us through your years of giving has afforded us the strength to move forward.

There is a temptation to rush to canonise(封……死者为圣徒) your memory; there is no need to do so. You stand tall enough as a human being of unique qualities not to need to be seen as a saint. Indeed, to sanctify(尊敬) your memory would be to miss out on the very core of your being, your wonderfully mischievous(淘气的) sense of humour with a laugh that bent you double. Your joy for life transmitted wherever you took your smile and the sparkle in those unforgettable eyes, your boundless energy which you could barely contain.

But your greatest gift was your intuition(直觉), and it was a gift you used wisely. This is what underpinned(巩固, 支撑) all your other wonderful attributes and if we look to analyze what it was about you that had such a wide appeal we find it in your instinctive feel for what was really important in all our lives. Without your God-given sensitivity we would be immersed(陷于) in greater ignorance at the anguish(痛苦, 苦恼) of AIDS and HIV sufferers, the plight(困境) of the homeless, the isolation of lepers(麻疯病患者), the random destruction of landmines. Diana explained to me once that it was her innermost feelings of suffering that made it possible for her to connect with her constituency(支持者, 赞助者) of the rejected. And here we come to another truth about her. For all the status, the glamour, the applause, Diana remained throughout a very insecure person at heart, almost childlike in her desire to do good for others so she could release herself from deep feelings of unworthiness of which her eating disorders were merely a symptom. The world sensed this part of her character and cherished her for her vulnerability whilst admiring her for her honesty.

Part VII Useful Words and Expressions

solemn state funeral	隆重的国葬
coffin	棺木
National cemetery	国家公墓
ashes	骨灰,遗体
bestow	把……赠与
bid the final farewell to sb.	向……遗体告别
corpse	尸体
cremation	火葬
crypt	地窖,教堂地下屋(作墓穴等用)
funeral committee	治丧委员会
funeral procession	送葬行列
hearse	柩车,灵车
last resting place	长眠之地
lie in state	尸体停放(供人瞻仰遗容)
mausoleum	陵墓
memorial park	陵园
mortuary	(丧葬前的)停尸室,(医院的)太平间,殡仪馆
pay (do) homage to	向……表示敬意
pay the final farewell to sb.	向……遗体告别
to be laid in rest	安葬
to fly a flag at half-mast	降半旗
urn	骨灰盒
vigil	守夜,祝祷仪式
wreath	花圈

keys for Lead-in Exercises

2. 1) A 2) J 3) I 4) G 5) C 6) H 7) D 8) F 9) E 10) B

***keys for Follow-up Practice* 1**

Person who attend the funeral	Family members of the departed
I'm sorry.	Thanks for coming.
My sympathy to you.	John talked about you often.
It was good to know John.	I didn't realize so many people cared.
John was a fine person and a friend of mine. He will be missed.	
Come see me when you can.	
My sympathy to your mother.	

Unit 7

The Etiquette of Business

Part I Lead-in Exercises

1. ***Do you know any business etiquette in western countries? If yes, please tell your classmates what you know about. If no, share with your classmates what you know about China's.***

2. ***Vocabulary building: Match the Chinese words on the left column with their appropriate English expressions on the right.***

1)欢迎宴会	A. Panel discussion
2)庆功宴	B. Welcome dinner
3)敬您一杯!	C. Presentation
4)举行谈判	D. Memorandum of understanding
5)双方商定的议程	E. Schedule mutually agreed upon
6)情况介绍	F. Glee feast
7)小组讨论	G. Keep close watch on
8)谅解备忘录	H. Here's to you!
9)密切注视	I. Enter into negotiation
10)不虚此行!	J. It's a rewarding trip!

1)________ 2)________ 3)________ 4)________ 5)________

6)________ 7)________ 8)________ 9)________ 10)________

3. ***Do you know how to behave in the following situations? Choose one you think appropriate and discuss with your partners why you choose them.***

1) One of the most ill-mannered things to do at a business meal is ________.

A. order a lot of food

B. smoke while the others are eating

C. set up business papers on the table

D. use a cell phone

2) When you have a business meeting in the UK, you should ________.

A. get down to business straight away

B. spend an hour introducing yourselves

C. avoid talking business immediately

D. spend time eating and drinking and getting to know each other

3) You have a meeting with a client but are expecting a call. You should ________.

A. make sure your cell phone is charged up and turned on

B. set your cell phone ring volume to high to ensure you hear any calls

C. turn your cell phone off

D. tell your client you are expecting a phone call

4) When you receive someone else's business card you should ________.

A. immediately put it into your back pocket

B. immediately pass them your business card

C. look at the card but say nothing about it

D. look at the card and acknowledge it

5) What should you do if you see someone at a business event that you have met before, but you can't remember their name?

A. ignore the person

B. introduce yourself, apologize for not remembering their name but say where you met them before

C. walk up to him or her and say, "Hi, mate!"

D. try to find out the person's name from others at the event and then introduce yourself.

6) When expressing thanks to a business client who has given you a gift, you should ________.

A. send an e-mail because it is faster and more efficient

B. send a handwritten note

C. call within 72 hours

D. a verbal thank you is enough

Part II Business Etiquette

"Etiquette would not seem to play an important part in business, and yet no man can ever tell when its knowledge may be of advantage, or its lack may turn the scale against him."—Emily Post, 1922

Although the face of business has changed drastically since 1922, when Emily Post wrote the words above, the secret power of etiquette is just as relevant today. Business etiquette is essentially about building relationships with colleagues, clients or customers. In the business world, it is these people that can influence your success or failure. Etiquette, and in particular business etiquette, is simply a means of maximizing your business potential by presenting yourself favorably.

1. *Making Appointments*

Prior appointments are necessary. Appointments should be made at least a few days in advance and, ideally, confirmed on arrival. Most businessmen in western countries tend to decline to meet a visitor even at relatively short notice.

It is best to avoid July and August when those with children are almost obliged to take their annual vacation. Easter is also popular for holidaying and there are two Bank Holidays in May that may catch the unwary visitor. Don't try to make an appointment between Christmas and New Year.

The easiest times of day to arrange an appointment are probably mid-morning and mid-afternoon. Breakfast meetings are rare and it is unlikely that an initial meeting will involve lunch (or dinner).

Punctuality is appreciated but no one really minds if you arrive a little late (up to 15 minutes) for a one-to-one meeting. Obviously, though, if several people are involved then there is a greater likelihood that someone will have another engagement to attend. On the other hand, you should not arrive too promptly for social events — but aim to arrive a respectable fifteen minutes after the specified time; thus, if a dinner invitation states "7:30 p. m. for 8:00 p. m.", it means that you will be expected at about 7:50 p. m.

2. *Business Dress*

Being appropriately dressed is essential in making good impressions in the business and corporate worlds. A polished image is important in business survival and can be an important factor in career advancement. In Unit 4, we have talked a lot about dressing etiquette; here some more specific tips will be centered on business dress.

- No matter what your age your Business attire should be as professional as possible. Avoid clothes that are the latest fashion and choose a more conservative look.
- Wear clothes that are comfortable, that do not ride up or bind. Dress to suit your personality while keeping in mind professional standards. When you feel comfortable you will feel more at ease and will be able to attend to Business.

- Your blouse should fit well. Be sure it is the correct size, is not tight and does not gap.
- Keep your hemline conservative, about one to two inches above the knee. This length is not only more attractive but a length that suits most women.
- Keep your business clothes clean and well pressed. If they should get stained have them cleaned immediately.
- Pinstripes are a classic business look and look best when the pinstripes are thin and widely spaced. Avoid thick stripes that are close together — this is a trendier

look and not appropriate for business.

- When attending business functions keep business cards in your pocket for easy access. This will allow you to present your card easily without having to search through handbags and briefcases. Remove the cards at the end of the day and keep them in a cardholder to ensure they stay in great shape.
- Do not over fill your briefcase or handbag and create a disorganized look. To carry files and business materials invest in a stylish, feminine looking bag.
- If you have an important meeting choose (and try on) the clothes you plan to wear beforehand. Finding that what you intended to wear is not what you expected could make you late or uncomfortable.

3. *Addressing Others with Respect*

Nowadays people are in fact quite informal and the immediate use of first names is increasingly prevalent in the western countries, especially amongst the young (under 40-45 years of age).

Nevertheless, you should always wait to be invited to use first names before doing so yourself. Quite often the invitation will be spontaneous but it may never happen at all. You should be careful to follow strict protocol, especially when dealing with older members of the "Establishment". No one is offended by exaggerated correctness whereas premature informality may be deemed presumptuous. The safe way is to follow the title given on a business card or the one given when first introduced.

The same principles apply to writing letters. You should start off formally and continue until your correspondent hints (e. g. by signing off with just his or her first name) that it is appropriate to switch. The rules for e-mail are more relaxed but there are some who write e-mails as if they were writing a "normal" letter.

4. *Office Etiquette*

Office etiquette are formal rules of behavior that make professional encounters pleasant and helpful. While certain procedures may seem awkward or wasteful to you as you begin working in a new environment, resist the urge to make immediate changes. The following are principles we should keep in mind:

- Discover how things are done and why. Observe how others answer the telephone, dress, decorate desks or office space, snack on the job, circulate memos, etc.

- Establish in your mind other people's priorities before asserting your own. Any changes you initiate will have more validity after you have familiarized yourself with the customary procedures.
- Whatever your position, a "thank you" is necessary, no matter how small the task or favor is.
- It is generally considered polite to hold a door open (or give it an extra push open) rather than let it slam in the face of someone following you. If someone opens or holds a door open for you, you must always thank them.

5. *Business Behaviors*

Business conversation may take place during meals. However, many times you will find more social conversation taking place during the actual meal.

Business meetings may be arranged as breakfast meetings, luncheon meetings, or dinner meetings depending on time schedules and necessity. Generally a dinner, even though for business purposes, is treated as a social meal and a time to build rapport.

If you do give a gift, it should not appear to be a bribe. An invitation for a meal or a modest gift is usually acceptable.

6. *Communications*

Offer a firm handshake, lasting 3-5 seconds, upon greeting and leaving. Maintain good eye contact during your handshake. If you are meeting several people at once, maintain eye contact with the person you are shaking hands with, until you are moving on the next person.

Good eye contact during business and social conversations shows interest, sincerity and confidence. Good friends may briefly embrace, although the larger the city, usually the more formal the behavior. Introductions include one's title if appropriate, or Mr., Ms, Mrs. and the full name. Business cards are generally exchanged during introductions. However, they may be exchanged when one party is leaving.

7. *Business Meeting*

Business meetings are one arena in which poor etiquette can have negative effects. By improving your business meeting etiquette you automatically improve your chances of success. Comfort, trust, attentiveness and clear communication are examples of the positive results of demonstrating good etiquette. Here are five tips to make sure you are a superstar in the meeting:

- Be on time. Be early. Arriving late is not only rude to your boss, your meeting leader, yourself, but it is also rude to the other participants. Why? Because it often requires attention being moved from the topic of discussion to the rude late-comer shuffling in.
- Avoid electronic distraction. Unless you are invited to record or take photos and videos of the discussion — keep your cellphones and other distractions turned off. If you need your PDA function for note taking — silence it.
- Prepare to be productive. If you were given a meeting agenda before hand study it and know your opinion on key points before the meeting begins. Know the news of the day and how it relates to your company, and the meeting topic. If called on, don't be afraid to take a beat to collect your thoughts before speaking your mind. The more prepared you are beforehand, the more you appear unflappable and an asset to the group.
- No signs of Gum. I don't care if you're on the latest "all gum" diet or not — the presenter should not be aware of your gum in a professional meeting. If they can notice it — it's rude. Do not be the attendee that disturbs the neighboring participants by opening candy and gum while the speaker is conducting the meeting.

- Pay attention as your career depends on it. Take notes and pay enough attention that you could sum up the key points for colleagues that were unable to attend. And really drink in the subjects that can be applied to your job functions.

Words and Expressions

unwary	*adj.* 不注意的，粗心的
attire	*n.* 服装，盛装
hemline	*n.* （裙子、衣服等的）底边，贴边
pinstripe	*n.* 细条子，线条，隐格布，细条子衣服
spontaneous	*adj.* 自发的
protocol	*n.* 外交礼节；礼仪，（条约）草案，草约；（外交）议定书
deem	*v.* 认为，相信
presumptuous	*adj.* 专横的
unflappable	*adj.* 不易惊慌的，镇定的
asset	*n.* 宝贵的人材，有利条件
premature	*adj.* 过早的
bribe	*n.* 贿赂

Part III Sample Dialogues

Sample Dialogue 1: Talking About Your Job

Jack: Hi, Peter. Can you tell me a little bit about your current job?
Peter: Certainly, What would you like to know?
Jack: First of all, what do you work as?
Peter: I work as a computer technician at Schuller's and Co.

Jack: What do your responsibilities include?
Peter: I'm responsible for systems administration and in-house programming.
Jack: What sort of problems do you deal with on a day-to-do basis?
Peter: Oh, there are always lots of small system glitches. I also provide information on a need-to-know basis for employees.
Jack: What else does your job involve?
Peter: Well, as I said, for part of my job I have to develop in-house programs for special company tasks.
Jack: Do you have to produce any reports?
Peter: No, I just have to make sure that everything is in good working order.
Jack: Do you ever attend meetings?
Peter: Yes, I attend organizational meetings at the end of the month.
Jack: Thanks for all the information, Peter. It sounds like you have an interesting job.
Peter: Yes, it's very interesting, but stressful, too!

Sample Dialogue 2: *Telephone Banking*

Representative: Hello. How can I help you today?
Customer: Hello. I'd like some information on the telephone banking services offered by your bank.
Representative: Certainly. What is your account number?
Customer: At the High Street Branch.
Representative: What would you like to know?
Customer: How do I sign up?
Representative: Just let me know, I'll sign you up immediately.
Customer: Can you tell me how the telephone banking services work?
Representative: You can do all your day-to-day banking over the telephone, 24 hours a day.
Customer: That's great. How do I access my account?
Representative: Just call the bank, key in your PIN number and listen to the menu of options available.
Customer: How do I choose which option I want?
Representative: Just press the number for the service stated by the recording.
Customer: What kind of things can I do?
Representative: You can check your balance, pay bills, order a statement or even transfer

money to another bank.

Customer: That's fantastic! Can I trade stocks and bonds?

Representative: I'm afraid you will have to have a special account for that.

Customer: What about getting help if I have any problems?

Representative: There's an automated answering machine and staff are available 9 to 5 seven days a week.

Customer: It all sounds very good to me. I'd like to sign up.

Representative: All right, can you answer a few questions please?

Customer: Certainly...

Sample Dialogue 3: At the Restaurant

(It's 12 o'clock. All staff leave their seats and go for working luncheon.)

Jack: Hei, Peter, It's time for lunch. Would you like to go with me? I'll show you the restaurant.

Peter: Sure, thank you.

(At the restaurant downstairs.)

Jack: This restaurant is open to the clerk working in this office building. Our company pays our lunch. First we should go to the corner to take a plate.

Jack: Then we go to that window.

Jack: You should tell the waiter what you would like to have.

Jack: I'd like some salad and —

Jack: Peter, it's your turn.

(Peter chooses some food he likes.)

Jack: Ok, let's go to find a seat.

(They hear a voice.)

Speaker: Hi, Jack, come here.

Jack: Hi, Terry and Kevin, this is Peter. He is new. And we work in the same department.

Jack: Peter, this is Terry, accountant. And this is Kevin. He is in marketing department.

Terry and Kevin: Nice to meet you.

Peter: Nice to meet you.

Sample Dialogue 4: Telephoning

Office assistant: Good morning. Odyssey Promotions. How may I help you?

Nick: Hello, this is Nick Delwin from Communicon. Could I speak to Helen Turner, please?

Office assistant: Just a moment, please.

Office assistant: I have Nick Delwin on the line for you.

Helen: Thank you... Hi, Nick. Nice to hear from you. How's the English weather?

Nick: It's pretty good for the time of year. What's it like in New York?

Helen: Not good, I'm afraid.

Nick: That's a pity because I'm planning to come across next week.

Helen: Really? Well, you'll come by to see us while you're here, I hope?

Nick: That's what I'm phoning about. I've got a meeting with a customer in Boston on Tuesday of next week. I was hoping we could arrange to meet up either before or after.

Helen: Great. That would give us a chance to show you the convention centre, and we could also drop in at Caesar's Restaurant where Gregg has arranged your reception.

Nick: That's what I was thinking.

Helen: So you said you have to be in Boston on Tuesday? That's the 8th?

Nick: That's right. Now, I could stop over in New York either on the way in—that would be the Monday... Would that be possible?

Helen: Ah, I'm afraid I won't be in the office on Monday, and I think Gregg has meetings all day.

Nick: Uh-huh, well, the other possibility would be to arrange it after Boston on my way home.

Helen: When do you plan on leaving Boston?

Nick: Could be either Tuesday afternoon or Wednesday morning, but I would like to catch a flight back to London on Wednesday evening.

Helen: OK. Well, it would be best for us if you could fly in on the Wednesday morning. Either Gregg or I will pick you up at the airport, and then we could show you the convention centre and also Caesar's. If there's time, you could come back to the office and we'll run through any of the details that still haven't been finalized.

Nick: That sounds good. Just as long as I can get back to the airport for my evening flight.

Helen: No problem. Look, why don't you fax me your information once you've confirmed your flight times? Then we'll get back to you with an itinerary for the day — that's Wednesday the 9th, right?

Nick: That's right. Good, well, I'll do that and I look forward to seeing you next week.

Helen: Same here. See you next week.

Part IV Follow-up Practice

1. ***Match the expressions of what they say in Column Ⅰ with what they mean in Column Ⅱ according to what you have got to know.***

Column Ⅰ	Column Ⅱ
What they say	What they mean
1) I didn't get your e-mail.	A. This is the way we have always done it.
2) We are following the standard.	B. Consumption is reduced when the power is off.
3) Maintenance free.	C. We are desperate and will try anything.
4) Energy saving.	D. We'll listen to what you have to say as long as it doesn't interfere with what we plan to do.
5) See me and let's discuss.	E. Impossible to fix.
6) Give us your interpretation.	F. The only guy who understood the thing quit.
7) Give us the benefit of your thinking.	G. I haven't checked my e-mail in days.
8) The entire concept will have to be abandoned.	H. I've screwed up again and need help.

2. ***Role play: Lin Ping is a new staff in an international organization. This is his first***

day working in the office. After the first day work, he is invited to attend a welcome party in the manager's home. Design a dialogue for him and his colleagues.

3. ***Work in pairs, making up dialogues according to the following situations.***
   - Inviting your business associate to dinner. (*accepting*)
   - Inviting your colleague to go on a tour to Hainan Island (*first declining, but accepting after persisting*).

Part V Reading for Fun

Casual Friday

Memo No. 1: Effective immediately, the company is adopting Fridays as Casual Day so that employees may express their diversity.

Memo No. 2: Spandex (用于腰带、游泳衣等的斯潘德克斯弹性纤维) and leather micro-miniskirts are not appropriate attire for Casual Day. Neither are string ties (蝶形领结) or moccasins (软拖鞋).

Memo No. 3: Casual Day refers to dress only, not attitude. When planning Friday's wardrobe (研究会), remember image is a key to our success.

Memo No. 4: A seminar on how to dress for Casual Day will be held at 4 p. m. Friday in the cafeteria. Fashion show to follow. Attendance is mandatory (强制的).

Memo No. 5: As an outgrowth of Friday's seminar, the Committee On Committees has appointed a 14-member Casual Day Task Force to prepare guidelines for proper dress.

Memo No. 6: The Casual Day Task Force has completed a 30-page manual. A copy of "Relaxing Dress Without Relaxing Company Standards" has been mailed to each employee. Please review the chapter "You Are What You Wear" and consult the "home casual" versus "business casual" checklist before leaving for work each Friday. If you have doubts about the appropriateness of an item of clothing, contact your CDTF representative before 7 a. m. on Friday.

Memo No. 7: Because of lack of participation, Casual Day has been discontinued, effective immediately.

Part VI Supplementary Reading

Failing to Observe Good Etiquette is Bad Manners, Bad for Business

Kansas City Business Journal—by Elizabeth Fountain

Since Confucius wrote the first rules of decorum, etiquette has been questioned, changed and argued as to its importance. Some argue the need for it, others want to know where to learn it and then there are people who ask why something is appropriate in one country and deemed totally unacceptable behavior in another part of the world. Finally, there are the little truisms(真实性)that all gentlemen were taught by their mothers, such as ladies first. In today's business arena, the "ladies first" rule could actually provoke a few women to incivility.

Knowing etiquette is becoming more important because these rules help guide us through a variety of situations in our ever-shrinking and changing world. All of us can attest(证实,证明)to situations in which, if we had known what do, it could have saved us embarrassment or even a job.

A favorite story is a dinner in Charleston, S. C. , where the saleswoman invited her very sophisticated client and his wife to dinner to celebrate the signing of a large construction contract. The owner of the Kansas City construction company insisted on going to the dinner with the saleswoman.

The saleswoman watched her commission dissipate(消失) while her boss picked his teeth with fish bones and impressed the party by using a commonly used expletive(感叹词,咒骂语) as five different parts of speech. Instead of using his dinner napkin to wipe his mouth, the boss wiped out the deal when he used it to blow his nose.

The following day the contract was rescinded(废除).

The boss was so intimidated(胆怯的,害怕的) by the refined people that he compensated for his lack of sophistication with a laissez faire(放任) attitude. In consequence, he ruined a lucrative(有利的) deal, tarnished(失去光泽) the image of his company and threw away the saleswoman's hard-earned commission.

Had he possessed some etiquette skills, all of this could have been avoided and everyone could have enjoyed a delightful evening, strengthening a business relationship.

Possessing good etiquette is also knowing when to put on the Ritz and when to do the Motel 6. There are situations where formalities would be totally out of place and viewed as ostentatious(装饰表面的，卖弄的) because the occasion calls for more casual behavior. Good examples of this are wearing a fur coat to do your grocery shopping or having your wife wear her jewels to a company picnic.

Snobbism is also bad etiquette. A group of people took a new associate to lunch. The newcomer felt compelled to do some one-upmanship(高人一等的作风) that backfired(事与愿违). When it was his turn to order, he asked the server if the sole on the menu was Dover Sole. Even though the server was extremely busy as the restaurant was packed with diners, he insisted that the server find out because he only eats Dover Sole.

The fish was of the Dover persuasion, so he ordered it. After tasting his entree, he commented that it was the best Dover Sole he had ever eaten.

Notes:

The Ritz: The world's greatest hotel, as conceived by the world's greatest hotelier. For over a century, The Ritz has been the benchmark by which other hotels are measured. A London landmark at 150 Piccadilly, The Ritz has been home to the great and the good, the intelligentsia, the glitterati and thousands of discerning guests since 1906.

Motel 6: Motel 6 is a major chain of budget motels in the United States and Canada, operated by Accor Hotels.

Tips to Help Make Your Job Interview Successful

Congratulations! Spending days, weeks, or possibly months of looking the right job has finally paid off and you've been asked to come in for an interview. Then comes the biggest question of all, "Now what?" You will only have 15 to 20 minutes to "sell" your experiences, attitude, and skills to the employer—most likely without knowing what the employer wants to hear from you. There are articles upon articles of advice on interviewing, from how to answer certain questions to how to dress—right down to the colour of your socks! It can seem overwhelming, but remembering a few key points can help make your interview successful.

● ***Research***

Find out a little bit about the company you want to work for. Visit the location in person if it is a store or building open to the general public. Visit the company's website and talk to anyone you might know who works there.

What kinds of products or services does the company make or sell? What types of people work there? What are the typical hours this position requires?

What are some of the day-to-day tasks that the job involves?

Make notes of things you want more information about and ask the employer about them at the end of your interview (it's always a good idea to have a few questions to ask the employer, anyway!). Researching a company and the position make you stand out in an interview. It shows that you are really interested in working there.

● ***Practice***

It sounds funny—and it looks even funnier — but practicing out loud for your interview will help you sound more polished and concise and less nervous in the actual interview. List a few key things you want the employer to know about you, and review common interview questions. Formulate answers to those questions and answer them out loud while looking at yourself in the mirror. This exercise prevents you from rambling in the interview and unpolished and unsure. It also helps you discover what really does the best candidate for the job!

● ***Dress to make a good first impression***

In an interview, first impressions do matter. The best way to ensure a good first impression is to dress smart. If you are interviewing for a job in an office, it is usually best to wear a dark-coloured, conservative suit (for both men and women). If you are interviewing for a job where the dress code is more casual (at a factory or a construction site, for example), nice slacks and a collared button-down shirt with a tie for men and a nice dress or blouse and slacks or skirt for women are usually appropriate. You should avoid wearing excessive jewellery, perfume, and flamboyant clothes. Good personal hygiene is also important.

If you are unsure what to wear, you should always go with the most conservative, professional option. Most experts agree it is better to be overdressed than dressed too casually. What you are wearing tells employers a lot about how serious you are about getting the job.

• ***Be conscious of good interview etiquette***

This list could go on forever—there is literally an endless array of "do's" and "don'ts" for an interview—and not everyone agrees on every aspect of that list. There are, however, some basic "interview etiquette" tips that are important to remember.

Be on time for your interview. This is, employers expect employees to arrive on time to work. They may see a person who is late to an interview, when he or she is supposed to be showing his or her best side, as someone who will have difficulty arriving on time to work or meeting deadlines if hired.

Be aware of your body language. When shaking hands, make sure your grip is firm and confident. Have good posture, but avoid appearing like you're as stiff as a cardboard cutout. Even the most experienced professionals get nervous in an interview—it's normal, However, if you appear too nervous, the interviewer might draw the wrong conclusions about your ability to do the job—especially if it involves interacting with people! Conversely, make sure you don't slouch—this could give the impression that you are lazy or uninterested in the position. Maintain eye contact with your interviewer to convey confidence. When speaking, be polite and professional and avoid using slang and profanities. The more confident and polished you appear the more likely you are to leave the interviewer with a positive impression of you.

Keep the interview positive. Avoid making negative remarks about any previous jobs or employers. Also, refrain from complaining about any job-related tasks or responsibilities you were given in a previous position. Employers want to hire someone who is positive, enthusiastic, and able to meet and deal with challenges.

• ***Be prepared to ask the interviewer questions***

This is where your research comes in. Employers want to know if you're truly interested in the position. They also want to know that you have all the information you need to make a decision, if offered the job. It isn't a good idea to turn the tables and "interview" the interviewer, but it is a good idea to go into the interview with a few questions in mind. This is your chance to ask additional questions about the business, the position, the requirements, and the expectations of the person who will fill the position.

All of this advice comes down to three important things to remember when you're interviewing: being prepared, professional, and polite is the best way to make the right impression!

Part VII Useful Words and Expressions

久仰!	I've heard so much about you.
好久不见了!	Long time no see.
辛苦了!	You've had a long day. You've had a long flight.
尊敬的朋友们	Distinguished/Honorable/Respected friends
我代表……欢迎各位朋友访问……	On behalf of …, I wish to extend our warm welcome to the friends who have come to visit …
我一定向他转达您的问候和邀请。	I'll surely remember you and your invitation to him.
欢迎美商来……投资。	American businessmen are welcome to make investment in …
欢迎多提宝贵意见。	Your valuable advice is most welcome.
我就不耽搁您了,您的日程很紧。	As you have a tight schedule, I will not take up more of your time.
请代我问候王先生。	Please remember me to Mr. Wang.
欢迎再来!	Hope you'll come again.
请留步,不用送了!	I will see myself out, please.
愿为您效劳!	At your service!
为……举行宴会/宴请	Host a dinner/banquet/luncheon in honor of …
便宴	Informal dinner
午宴	Luncheon
便餐	Light meal
答谢宴会	Return dinner
告别宴会	Farewell dinner
招待会	Reception
鸡尾酒会	Cocktail party

茶话会	Tea party
上菜	Serve a course
您的位置在这里。	Here is your seat.
请入席!	Please make have a seat.
欢聚一堂	Enjoy this happy get-together
请随便!	Please make yourself at home. /Please enjoy yourself.
最后,我借主人的酒,提议为……干杯!	Lastly, taking up this glass of fine wine, I propose a toast to …
请各位举杯并同我一起为所有在座的朋友们的健康干杯!	I'd ask you to raise your glass and join me in a toast to the health of all our friends present here.
我要为此干杯!	I'll drink to that!
随量!	Whatever you like!
招待会现在开始。	The reception will now begin.
出席今天招待会的贵宾有……	The distinguished guests participating the reception are …
现在请……讲话	I have the honour to call upon …
举行会议/研讨会/大会/座谈会/学术报告会	Hold a meeting/seminar/conference/forum/symposium
赞助人/主办人/承办人/协办人	Patron/sponsor/organizer/co-organizer
交涉	Make representations with sb. on sth. /deal with sb.
事物性会谈	Talks at working level
对口会谈	Counterpart talks
议程项目	Items on the agenda
议题	Topic for discussion
全体会议	Plenary session
开场白	Introduction
同有关单位磋商	Hold consultations with the organizations concerned

一轮会谈	One round of talks
决议	Resolution
现在开会。	I declare the meeting open.
请……发言。	I invite the representative of ... to take the floor.
我要说的就是这些。	That's all for what I want to say.
您看是先谈原则问题呢,还是先谈具体问题?	I wonder if you would like to start with matters of principle or specific issues?
在谈那个问题之前我想对您刚才讲的话谈点看法。	Before we turn to that issue, I wish to make a few comments/remarks on your presentation.
您对此事怎么看呢?	I wish to benefit from your views on this matter. /What is your view on this matter? / How do you see this matter?
我提议休会十分钟。	I propose a 10-minute break.
纠缠这个问题。	Entangle this issue.
经受了时间考验的友谊给我留下了很深的印象。	The time-tested friendship leaves me a deep impression.
促进密切合作	Spur/promote intensive cooperation

Keys for Lead-in Exercises

2\. 1)B 2)F 3)H 4)I 5)E 6)C 7)A 8)D 9)G 10)J

3\. 1)D 2)A 3)C 4)D 5)B 6)B

Follow-up practice 1

1)G 2)A 3)E 4)B 5)D 6)C 7)H 8)F

Unit 8

The Taboos in Western Culture and Etiquette

Part I Lead-in Exercises

1. ***Have you ever heard or read some stories about taboos in western culture? If yes, share your experience with your partners.***
2. ***Have you ever met with some very embarrassing moment when you get along with westerners because of your ignorance of taboo culture?***
3. ***Background building:***

• Do you know what relationship between "taboo" and "tapu"?

"Taboo" is a ritually sanctioned prohibition against contact with a thing, a person or an activity. The word itself originated in Polynesia, where taboo played an important cultural role, but the concept is universal. The use of the word "taboo" is drawn from "tapu," meaning "not allowed," and traces back to the year 1777 and the English explorer Captain James Cook, visiting a place he named "the Friendly Islands" (now Tonga).

• Do you know the difference between "taboo" and "superstition"?

Taboo: it means a prohibition, excluding something from use, approach, or mention because of its sacred and inviolable nature, or a ban or an inhibition resulting from social custom or emotional aversion.

Superstition: it means a belief, practice, or rite irrationally maintained by ignorance of the laws of nature or by faith in magic or chance; or irrational belief that an object, an action, or a circumstance not logically related to a course of events influences its outcome.

Notes:

But sometimes, the concept of taboo and superstition can interlace with one another, for example, the people's attitude toward the number "13" in western countries.

Part II Some Knowledge about Taboo

A taboo is a strong social prohibition (or ban) against words, objects, actions, or discussions that are considered undesirable or offensive by a group, culture, society, or community. Breaking a taboo is usually considered offensive. Some taboo activities or customs are prohibited by law and transgressions may lead to severe penalties. Other taboos result in embarrassment, shame and rudeness. That's why it is necessary for us to know some basic taboos in the western world to avoid awkward situations in communication.

1. *Taboo Food*

- ***Amphibians and reptiles***

Both Judaism and Islam strictly forbid the consumption of amphibians such as frogs and reptiles such as crocodiles and snakes. Nevertheless, frogs are raised commercially in certain countries and frog legs are considered a delicacy in France, Portugal, China, Caribbean and in parts of the USA and India.

- ***Birds***

The Old Testament of the Bible explicitly states that the eagle, vulture, and osprey are not to be eaten. Interestingly, bats are also included in this list of "birds". Large domesticated fowl such as chickens, turkeys, and ducks are commonly eaten in many cultures, along with their wild game counterparts.

Pigeons are raised and eaten in parts of the Middle East, Asia and Europe, where the young birds are known as "squab". In North America, pigeons (as doves) are a hunted game bird in many areas, however, urban pigeons are considered unfit for consumption.

Many people also find the thought of eating the meat of crows and other scavengers repulsive, as evidenced by the expression "eating crow". Eating swans is generally considered unacceptable in Europe and the Americas, and the swan is a protected bird in England. All mute swans in Britain belong to the sovereign, Queen Elizabeth Ⅱ, a historical quirk dating from the twelfth century.

Small birds such as songbirds have also traditionally been eaten in the Middle East, Asia and some European cultures. In Western cultures today, most people regard songbirds as backyard wildlife rather than as food. In addition, some migratory birds are protected by international treaty.

• ***Deer/Reindeer***

Although reindeer is popular as a dish in Alaska, Norway, Sweden, Finland, Russia and Canada, many people in the United Kingdom and Ireland are squeamish about the idea of eating reindeer meat. This relates to the popular culture myth of the reindeer as assistant to Father Christmas, as opposed to the "cows of the north" vision of the Northern countries.

• ***Cats***

In Guangdong, China, cat is reportedly served along with snake and chicken in a dish called "The Dragon, Tiger and Phoenix". In desperate times, people have been known to resort to cooking and eating cats, in places where it is otherwise not usual to do so.

Cats are sometimes confused with civet cats, which are not felines at all. This has led Americans to accuse some countries' manufacturers of using cat fur in their products. In 2001, a shipment of cat toys imported into the United States were recalled and destroyed because they were trimmed with cat fur, which had just been banned in the U. S.

- ***Veal***

Some people, especially in Britain, Ireland, Canada and United States of America, choose not to eat veal (the meat of young cattle) due to concerns about inhumane treatment of the calves. In the UK, this taboo is waning (减弱) due to a 2007 EU directive banning veal crates and anemia-inducing diets.

- ***Dogs***

In a number of countries around the world, apart from being kept as pets, certain breeds of dogs are slaughtered as a source of meat and specifically raised on farms for that purpose. According to the ancient Hindu scriptures, *dog's meat* was regarded as the most unclean (and rather poisonous) food possible—it was worthy only for the lowest of the untouchable castes — who were therefore called *śvapaca* (those cooking dog's meat).

Paying more attention to the people who keep dogs as pets, we never treat them with the meat of dogs.

- ***Horses***

The eating of horse meat is a food taboo to most people in the United Kingdom, the US, and Australia, and its supply is sometimes even illegal. In the UK, this strong taboo includes banning horsemeat from commercial pet food and DNA testing of some types of salami suspected of containing donkey meat. Like lobster and dog, it is forbidden in Judaism, Hinduism, and some sects of Christianity.

Horse meat was sold in the US during WW Ⅱ, since beef was expensive, rationed and destined for the troops. The primary concern of the authorities at the time was to prevent it being marketed to the unwary as beef. However, it is fairly common in Scandinavia and parts of continental Europe, and is considered a delicacy in Japan, where it is also eaten raw as a type of sashimi.

- ***Insects***

Except for certain locusts and related species, insects are not considered suitable for

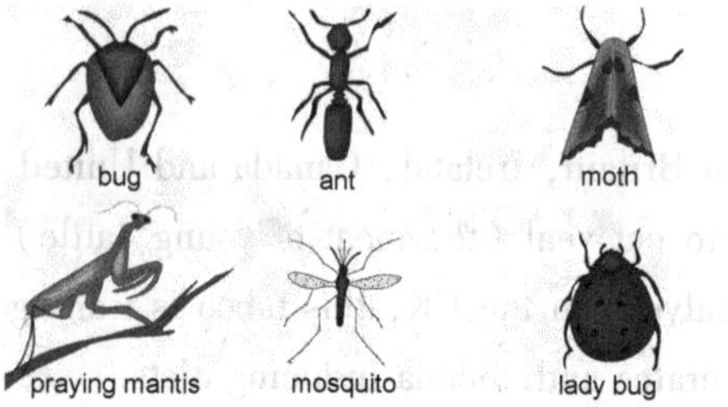

eating. Generally speaking, insects have been prevented form consuming as food in European cultures. But the taboos against insects as a food source generally do not apply to honey (concentrated nectar which has been regurgitated by bees). Many vegetarians avoid honey as they would any other animal product.

- ***Living animals***

Western culture forbids any portion that is cut from a live animal. Even in cultures that do not prescribe ritual methods of livestock slaughter, the consumption of animals that are still alive is often seen as barbarity.

Another notable exception is shrimp. In Shanghai, China, and surrounding areas, live shrimp is a common dish served both in homes and restaurants. The shrimp are usually served in a bowl of alcohol, which makes the shrimp sluggish and complacent. Local belief is that live shrimp are "healthier" than those served "already dead" or cooked.

- ***Offal***

Offal is a traditional part of many European and Asian cuisines, including such dishes as the well-known steak and kidney pie in the United Kingdom. In countries such as Australia, Canada and the United States, on the other hand, many people are squeamish about eating offal. In these countries, organ meats that are considered edible in other cultures are more often regarded as fit only for processing into pet food under the euphemism "meat by-products". Except for liver (chicken, beef, or pork), and intestines used as natural sausage casings, organ meats consumed in the U.S. tend to be regional or ethnic specialties.

- ***Rats and mice***

In most Western cultures, rats and mice are considered either unclean vermin or pets and thus unfit for human consumption, traditionally being seen as carriers of plague. However, rats are commonly eaten in rural Thailand, Vietnam and other parts of

Indochina.

Historically, rats and mice have also been eaten in the West during times of shortage or emergency, such as during the Battle of Vicksburg and the Siege of Paris. In France, rats bred in the wine stores of Gironde were cooked with the fire of broken wine barrels and eaten.

- ***Snails***

Snails have been eaten for thousands of years, beginning in the Pleistocene. As they are mollusks, snails are neither kosher nor halal. They are especially abundant in Capsian sites in North Africa but are also found throughout the Mediterranean region in archaeological sites dating between 12,000 and 6,000 years ago. They are also seen a notable delicacy in France and other Mediterranean countries. However, in Britain, Ireland, and America, eating them may be seen as disgusting. Some English-speaking commentators have used the French word for snails, *escargot*, as an alternative word for snails, particularly snails for consumption.

- ***Vegetables***

Although it isn't a taboo in a strictest sense, many Germans, in particular older Germans, will not eat Swede (swedish turnip, rutabaga), as they see it as a "famine food", not for general consumption. This taboo existed from the 1916-1917 famine (*Steckrübenwinter*) when Germany had one of the worst winters in memory, where often the only food available was swedes. This led distaste to the vegetable which still continues today.

2. *Taboo Drinks*

- ***Alcohol***

Some religions—most notably Hinduism, Islam, Baptists and other Evangelical Christians—forbid or discourage the consumption of alcoholic beverages.

• *Blood*

Drinking blood is a strong taboo in many countries, and is often vaguely associated with vampirism (the consumption of human blood).

Although blood sausage, or blood made into cake form, is quite popular in many parts of the world, it is considered repulsive in most of the United States. In Britain and some Commonwealth countries, "black pudding" or "blood pudding" is made from blood. Followers of Judaism and Islam are forbidden to drink blood or eat food made from blood.

3. *Taboo Number*

• *Six*

In western culture, especially in Christian world, number "six" is an evil number. In the Bible, asserts 666 to be "the number of evil", associated with the beast, an antagonistic creature. In modern popular culture, 666 has become one of the most widely recognized symbols for Satan or the Devil. Earnest references to 666 occur both among apocalypticist Christian groups and in explicitly anti-Christian subcultures such as that surrounding some heavy metal bands; more humorous allusions to the 666 symbolism.

• *Thirteen*

In the west, number "13" is always unlucky, always indicating occurrence of disaster or symbol of misfortune. It is mainly to come from a religion: Jesus was betrayed by Judas, and made a great sacrifice; they totally are 13 people. And that is exactly Friday, so if the 13th plus Friday, it will be thought to be a very dangerous day. In the meantime, in ancient Greece, Hesiod was virtuous to warn farmer not to cultivate on the 13th. In West of medieval times ages, the scaffold was certain to have 13 steps, and the salary of executioner had 13 pieces of gold coin.

• *Odd and even number*

The western people see the even number as the symbol of misfortune, but the odd numbers as a good luck of symbol. The Russian believe odd number means happiness, the even number indicates disaster. And therefore, the wedding to send flowers is odd number, but the even number on funeral. British people hatching chicken to take to the hen of egg always are odd number. If you take the even number, it means a meeting to grow worse, or keep not good chicken. By the way, many west people like to use odd numbers price when doing business.

4. *Taboo Color*

• *Yellow*

Yellow is a bright and cheerful color. But in the English language, yellow is associated with jaundice and cowardice. In American slang, a coward is said to have a "yellow belly". It can also mean that something is tainted, as in the expression "yellow journalism". In English culture, yellow makes people think of Judas, who betrayed Jesus, because in the western painting, Judas is always portrayed as wearing yellow dress.

In America, yellow contains expectation, missing, and yearning for return of their far-away relatives. When the American hostage detained by Iran returned to country, the American raised the yellow paper, yellow silk, adoring the yellow memorial chapter to welcome them.

• *Black*

Black is a basic taboo of color in English culture and is most often used with negative connotation. Black is often the color of mourning. Historically, widows and widowers were expected to wear black for a year after the death of their spouses. In these cultures, the color black is often used in painting, film, and literature to evoke a sense of the fear or to symbolize death.

At the same time, in Western fashion, black is considered reliably stylish. Black suit and black dress are most favored. The colloquialism "the new black" is a reference to the latest trend or fad. On important occasions, all people like to wear black; the member of the symphony orchestra is almost all in black suit.

5. *Verbal taboo*

- ***Sacrilegious Taboos***

In Western countries, some Christians believe that it is disrespectful for the misuse of God or God's name. Christians are forbidden to "take the Lord's name in vain" and this prohibition has been extended to the use of curses, which are believed to have magical powers. Thus hell and damn are changed to heck and darn, perhaps with the belief or hope that this change will fool the "powers that be". In the world of Harry Potter, the evil Voldmort is not to be named, but is referred to as "You-Know-Who".

- ***Abusive Taboos***

From the primitive society to the modern society, some abusive words are forbidden by the general public. Some animal names are used to abuse someone, such as bitch, cow, swine. Such words are called four-letter words. In modern society, people are still very sensitive to use these four-letter words, although they have right to do it. Now, people advocate the civilized and polite exchange, which shows up in different cultures. To communicate successfully, people are advised to avoid these abusive words to avoid embarrassment.

- ***Obscene Taboos***

Words relating to sex and sex organs make up a large part of the set of taboo words in many cultures. Some languages have no native words to mean "sexual intercourse". Other languages have many words for this common and universal act, most of which are taboo.

- ***Taboos of Disease and Death***

It is a natural process of "old, sick and die". It is to be a taboo topic because of people's fear for death. For example, people wouldn't directly talk about cancer because they fear that the cancer has and care about the feelings of the sufferer. English tends to be used "the long illness" to avoid using "cancer". When someone dies , people just use "pass away", "be on more", etc.

But taboo is not immutable. With the development of society, a lot of verbal taboos have been changed. For example:

◇She has cancelled all her social engagement. (1856)

◇She is in an interesting condition. (1890)

◇She is in a family way. (1920)

◇She is expecting. (1935)

◇She is pregnant. (1956)

We can easily find that pregnancy, which was considered taboo from the 1856, was mentioned after 100 years. Therefore, the taboo is a relative concept.

There are a lot of behavior taboos in western culture, which have been covered in the previous units. So here the space will be not be spared to describe them.

Words and Expressions

transgressions	*n.* 违反，犯罪
penalty	*n.* 处罚，罚款
amphibian	*adj.* 两栖类的，水陆两用的；*n.* 两栖动物
reptile	*n.* 爬虫动物，卑鄙的人；*adj.* 爬虫类的，卑鄙的
vulture	*n.* 秃鹰，贪婪的人
explicitly	*adv.* 明白地，明确地
osprey	*n.* 鱼鹰
fowl	*n.* 家禽，禽，禽肉
crow	*n.* 乌鸦
squab	*adj.* 刚孵出的，羽毛未丰的；*n.* 雏鸟
scavenger	*n.* 食腐动物
repulsive	*adj.* 排斥的，令人厌恶的
Mute swan	*n.* (动)疣鼻天鹅
sovereign	*n.* 君主，统治
quirk	*n.* 怪癖

reindeer	*n.* 驯鹿
squeamish	*adj.* 过于拘谨的，洁癖的，易呕吐的，神经质的
civet cats	*n.* 麝猫，灵猫
feline	*adj.* 猫的，猫科的；*n.* 猫科的动物
veal	*n.* 小牛肉，幼小的菜牛
anemia	*n.* 贫血，贫血症
inhumane	*adj.* 残忍的
slaughter	*n.* 屠宰，残杀，屠杀
Hindu	*n.* 印度教教徒；*adj.* 印度人的，印度教的
salami	*n.* 意大利腊肠
ration	*n.* 定量配给；*v.* 配给，分发，实行定量配给
destine	*vt.* 注定，预定
sashimi	*n.*（日）生鱼片
nectar	*n.* 花蜜，甘露
regurgitate	*v.*（使）涌回，（使）反刍
prescribe	*v.* 指示，规定，处（方），开（药）
barbarity	*n.* 残暴的行为，残忍
sluggish	*adj.* 行动迟缓的
complacent	*adj.* 自满的，得意的
offal	*n.* 碎屑，残渣，（猪、牛、羊等屠宰后的）头，尾，下水
squeamish	*adj.* 洁癖的，易呕吐的，神经质的
edible	*adj.* 可食用的
intestine	*adj.* 内部的，国内的；*n.*（解，动）肠

euphemism	*n.* (语法)委婉的说法
Pleistocene	*n.* (地)更新世，洪积世
mollusk	*n.* (动)软体动物
halal	*n.* 伊斯兰教律法的合法食物
archaeological	*adj.* 考古学的，考古学上的
swede	*n.* 蕉青甘蓝
Baptist	*n.* 施洗者，浸信会教友
Evangelical	*n.* 信福音主义者
antagonist	*n.* 敌手，对手
Satan	*n.* 撒旦，魔鬼
apocalypticist	*n.* 预言大灾难降临的人
allusion	*n.* 提及，暗示
virtuous	*adj* 善良的，有道德的，贞洁的
scaffold	*n.* 绞刑台
executioner	*n.* 死刑执行人，刽子手
jaundice	*n.* (医)黄疸
cowardice	*n.* 怯懦，胆小
taint	*v.* 感染
yearn	*vi.* 渴望，想念，怀念，向往
connotation	*n.* 含蓄，含蓄的东西(词、语等)，内涵
sacrilegious	*adj.* 冒渎的，该受天谴的
abusive	*adj.* 辱骂的，滥用的
obscene	*adj.* 淫秽的，猥亵的

intercourse	*n.* 交往，交流
evoke	*vt.* 唤起，引起，博得
untanned	*adj.* 未晒黑
lavatorial	*adj.* 低级粗俗的
baptism	*n.* 浸洗；(喻)洗礼，严峻考验
spectrum	*n.* 光，光谱，型谱
equilibrium	*n.* 平衡，均衡，保持平衡的能力

Part III Sample Dialogues

Sample Dialogue 1: *At a Restaurant*

Waiter: Good evening, welcome to Dream Hotel. Can I help you?

Yang: Yes, I would like to have a table near the window for enjoying the river view when we have a dinner.

Waiter: Certainly, this way please.

Yang: Thank you, boy.

(Way to the window table.)

Waiter: Here is the menu for this week. I will come back and take your order within a few minutes.

Yang: Thanks a million. Er, Jack, would you like to try something?

Jack: No, I am not good at it, and I don't understand Chinese words.

Yang: Er, here the fried frog is very good, and I tried before, okay?

Jack: Wow, I know some Chinese like frogs, but…, but you know, my wife, she is adherent to Judaism, so…

Yang: Gee, sorry, I forgot, we can get some beefsteak.

Jack: Great! we can try some fish, the grilled one, that's delicious.

Yang: And some roast chicken…

(Laugh …)

Sample Dialogue 2: On Yang's Evening Party

Nicola: Hi, so nice, I am really full, up here, look! Yang prepares so much beautiful food for us. Great buffet! Great birthday party!

Mouhamed: Well, I think so, but I can not eat this, this, and that.

Nicola: Sorry, you mean… you are hungry now.

Mouhamed: No, no, in my country we can not eat this fish, pork, and that one; I think it's still pork.

Nicola: Yeah, I see. Here you can find some beef.

Mouhamed: Yes, that the only meat I have to eat tonight.

Nicola: Would you like to try some alcohol?

Mouhamed: No, no, I just try a little beer, just a little.

Nicola: How about vegetable?

Mouhamed: That's perfect, and the salad.

Sample Dialogue 3: Visiting Simon's Family

Jack: Hi, Yang, are you free tomorrow?

Yang: Yeah, what?

Jack: Simon's girlfriend called over to see him, and Simon wants to have a party in his house.

Yang: Perfect, I know Simon has some great wine.

Jack: Well, I know, it's really mouthwatering. Tomorrow afternoon, 4 o'clock.

Yang: I will be there on time. By the way, shall we take some gifts for them?

Jack: Good idea. But what does she like? She is a girl, you know. Every 14th Jan I have to rack my brains day and night.

Yang: Me too! Can we send her some flowers? Girls always like it.

Jack: Well, agree with you.

Yang: I'll go to the flower shop opposite our school tomorrow.

Jack: Please remember to buy seven, or nine, or eleven bouquets.

Yang: Why? For what?

Jack: Because Simon's sweetheart, Vera Ilyina, she is from Russia.

Sample Dialogue 4: Planning a Trip

Yang: Simon, Nicola, Vera, everybody, meeting now!

Jack: Yeah, Spring break is coming, how about your idea?

Vera: Where will we go this time?

Nicola: How about the castle? I mean that one built in 13th century on the mountain.

Simon: Great, that one, I know, very spooky, wow, wow... .

(Simon makes faces.)

Vera: Shut up, it's not funny.

Yang: Yeah, yesterday I saw Alfred Hitchcock's *The Shining*. It's really...

Jack: But it's very exciting.

Nicola: Yes, we are young man, we have five persons. And Simon's uncle has a gun!

Simon: Exactly, I can bring, see. We go! Who wants to quit?

Yang: Right, I go with you. Next Friday? Because on Sunday I will be back to China.

Vera: No... , next Friday is 13th. Never, never! If you do that day, I stay at home.

(Everybody looks at each other and say...)

All: Tomorrow.

Part IV Follow-up Practice

1. ***Role Play**: Your friend is planning to study in USA as homestay, would you give him or her some suggestion when living with Americans?*

2. ***Group Work**: This is an international traveling group, and each of you will be a guide from different areas in this world. Please introduce some taboos in your own culture in order to let your tourists know something before.*

Student A is from America.

Student B is from France.

Student D is from China.

3. ***Discussion*: *List different taboos in China and compare them with that in western culture.***

Part V Reading for Fun

Taboo of Space

Jack had just arrived from the United States to study engineering at a Chinese university. In the first few days he met and moved in with his roommate Yang and met several of the students who lived in nearby dormitory rooms. Most of them were also studying engineering but had little experience with Americans. He usually went to the student cafeteria with them and they were very helpful in showing him around and in gently correcting his classroom Chinese.

One evening he settled in for his study in his room. After a time Yang left to visit another room where friends were listening to a radio broadcast. Jack said he would join him later. When Jack decided to take a break and see what the "guys" were up to, he found Yang and two other boys huddled（挤作一团）over the radio. Jack found it quite odd; however, that Yang was draped（懒散地放着）over the back of the boy seated in front of the radio. Moreover, that boy had his feet propped（支撑）up on his roommate who was seated nearby. It seemed to Jack that he had startled them, since they jumped up and welcomed him and even offered him tea. After Jack had a cup of tea and a chair to sit in, the group returned to the radio.

Jack shrugged the incident off, but over the next few days noticed that female students on campus frequently walked arm-in-arm or even holding hands. He noticed, too, that students of both sexes, but especially the boys, would huddle around newspaper displays in a fashion of close contact similar to Yang and others around the radio. Jack felt rather uncomfortable and wondered how he would respond if one of his classmates were to put his arms around him.

Part VI Supplementary Reading

To Touch or Not to Touch

Researchers classify Americans as low touchers in relation to other people of the world. However, touch in a multicultural society is very individual.

- You will meet some people who will never touch you, even though they highly prize your friendship. And you will meet others who will touch you often, usually on the shoulders and arms, but such touches will not really express a meaning.
- Because US society is very aware of the potential for people to use negative touch to intimidate or threaten, people are careful in how they touch.
- In the US, touch is used mainly as a greeting or to say goodbye.
- Americans can give the feeling of touch (without touching) by allowing others to move in close when talking.
- Good friends may exchange hugs, friendly punches, kisses, and may touch frequently when talking to each other.
- For acquaintances and superiors, like professors or interviewers, a simple handshake is all that is expected.
- Some people are high touchers and give friendly arm, back and shoulder touches even to new acquaintances.
- You will find that some students feel free to show in public what might be considered "private" expressions of affection in your culture. An example might be kissing outside classrooms.

Space Is Jealously Guarded

Privacy is the key to understanding the use of space and territory in the US.

- Americans claim, use, and will defend what is their chair, their television, their stereo, or their kitchen.
- Most interpersonal disagreements between roommates focus around the use of space and the idea of ownership. For instance:

◇He drank my milk from my side of the refrigerator!

◇She used my stapler and kept it on her desk.

◇They just walked in and turned on my stereo without asking.

◇He took five drawers for his clothes and left me just two!

- US students feel free to decorate their environments if they have "paid" for them through rent or dorm fees.
- In general, Americans are generous people who will lend and give freely of possessions, but only to those who ask first.
- Even in public places (library or large dorm lounge), people often "mark" their space by putting down a piece of clothing (coat), books or food to show that, "This place is mine and I'll be right back, Don't come here."
- Doors send messages. In almost all cases, the open door says "I'm friendly," and the closed door suggests "I'd rather be alone", You might shut your door only because you want to study, but you should be aware that others may see that shut door and, fairly or not, assume it represents your whole attitude or personality.
- Americans are very aware of scents(气味，香味) and smells, judging others and their dwellings(住处) by the type and intensity of scents detected. Windows and doors are usually kept wide open to let in "the fresh air."

Friday the 13th: The History of Friday Taboos and Superstition

The fear of Friday the 13th is a popular superstition. Examples of the taboos for both Friday and the number 13 are numerous.

Friday's ill-fated superstitious connotations are believed to result from the idea that it was the day of the week on which Eve tempted Adam and Christ was crucified(十字架上钉死).

Among the activities that are taboo on a Friday: setting sail on a ship; moving house; beginning any new work; writing a letter; knitting; starting a journey; and cutting your nails. In both England and America the custom to hang criminals on a Friday earned it the reputation of Hangman's day.

One activity offers some promise on a Friday—sleeping. The thought is, if you repeat the dream you had during the night to a family member on Friday morning, the dream will come true.

Not everywhere does Friday have this dubious distinction. Friday is the Sabbath of the Jewish lunar calendar and the Sabbath of Islam. Scandinavian Pagans, Hindus, rural Scots, and Germans consider Friday a fertile day, favourable for a marriage or courting. Their more favorable view of Friday is a result of the history of Friday before Christianity.

Friday is the only day of the week named after a woman. The others pay homage to either Scandinavian male gods (Wooden, Thor, and Tiu — God of War) or celestial(天体的) bodies (Saturn, Sun, and Moon). Friday was named after the Norse Goddess Freya who represented fertility and sexual love. She is strongly associated with spring, birds and cats.

Romans named the day dies Veneris after Venus, their own version of the Freya goddess. Ancient fisherman did not set sail on a Friday out of respect for Freya, because she was Goddess of the Sea. This tradition is still practiced by sea folk today, except the reluctance to set sail on a Friday is now due to a fear of bad luck.

The number 13 has an even more special place in superstition and fear of its effects has even been given a scientific name, Tridecaphobia. In fact, buildings avoid numbering the 13th floor, and airlines avoid using the number in tracking their flights and in numbering their seat aisles. The number 13 is rarely found on offices or shops, and even less frequently on the rooms of a hotel or guesthouse. In some cities, such as Paris, scarcely a single house exists with that ill-fated number. They get around this by designating the property twelve bis (twelve twice).

The main reason given for 13's ill omen(预兆、征兆) is its association with the Last Supper, attended by 13—Christ and the 12 apostles. According to tradition, if a gathering of 13 is held, one member of such a group — the first to rise from the table—will die before the year is out. Reportedly, an organization in France exists solely(独自地，单独地) to provide a last minute party guest so 13 people are never at a dinner party! Again, as was the case for Friday, not all cultures share this dislike for the number 13. For example, the Chinese have no aversion(厌恶，讨厌的事和人) to the number 13 because its literal meaning is "alive". Their taboo number, however, is four, because it sounds like the word for "dying" or "death".

Two conflicting calendars were in use during most of the early Christian era in Europe. The Church's official solar Julian Calendar (the one we use today) and the peasants unofficial lunar calendar. When the number 13 is examined in a little more depth, a strong pagan (异教徒) and even stronger female pattern emerges. Paganism centers around Mother Nature and, within that context, the moon is vital. The moon and female fertility are also closely connected. The connection is so strong in fact that it is generally believed calendar consciousness developed first in women, because the natural menstruation of their bodies correlated with the moons phases. The 13 lunar months gave 364 days per year (13×28) with one extra day to make up the solar calendar. Nursery rhymes, fairy tales, ballads, and other repositories of pagan tradition always describe the full annual solar cycle as a year and a day. Thus, the thirteen months of the fertility or lunar year led to the pagan reverence for the number 13 and probably led to the Christian dislike of it.

Part VII Useful Words and Expressions

Expressions to express anger and calm sb. down:

- What a nuisance!
- I've just have enough of it!
- What a stupid idiot!
- It makes me sick the way they talk to the little kids.
- Why the hell don't they just go away!
- Take it easy!
- Don't you think you're over-reacting a bit?
- There's no need to get so upset.
- It's not as bad as all that.
- I'm sorry to hear that.

Expressions to express indifference and the response:

- I couldn't care less.
- I don't mind what you do.
- The whole thing bores me to death.
- It doesn't matter to me.

- It's a bore, as far as I'm concerned.
- It's not as bad as all that, surely?
- Listen, if you look at it this way…
- Oh, come on, it's actually quite interesting.
- I see what you mean, but on the other hand…

***Expressions to express disappointment and the response*:**

- I was really looking forward to a more wonderful performance.
- It is really a shame that he talked to us so rudely.
- It's such a pity that I cannot attend your wedding ceremony.
- I'm really disappointed that the party will be held on next Friday.
- I wish I could have another four years at college.
- Oh, calm down. It can't be helped.
- It is not so bad as you thought.
- Don't worry. We can show you the video after you come back.

***Expressions to make a date and the response*:**

- Are you free this evening, by any chance?
- I was thinking of going to the cinema this evening, would you like to come?
- I'm going out to the theatre with some friends. Would you like to join us?
- That'd be lovely.
- I'd love to.
- How nice of you, thanks very much.
- Mmm, that's a great idea.
- Oh, I'm afraid I'm busy tonight.
- Tonight's difficult. Perhaps tomorrow evening, OK?
- This evening is a bit of a problem. What about tomorrow?

参考文献

[1]陈苏东,陈建平,唐桂民,等．商务英语听说[M]．北京:高等教育出版社,2003.

[2]迟振航．英美习俗与社交礼仪[M]．辽宁人民出版社,1985.

[3]杜学增．中英文化习俗比较[M]．外语教学与研究出版社,1999.

[4]高福进．西方人的习俗礼仪及文化[M]．上海辞书出版社,2003.

[5]兰素萍,蒋红．华中科技大学外语系编著《新世纪大学英语.英美文化视听教程》[M]．武汉:华中科技大学出版社,2002.

[6]李红,陈丹．敢说礼仪英语[M]．机械工业出版社,2005.

[7]李惠中．跟我学礼仪[M]．中国商业出版社,2002.

[8]李兆平,朱建新．说家常[M]．北京:华文出版社,2002.

[9]玉华,彭翠萍,武倩．英语阅读精华——风土人情篇[M]．东华大学出版社,2004.

[10]赵擎天．即学即用礼仪英语[M]．北京:中国纺织出版社,2002.